Needle Felting
by Hand or Machine

Linda Turner Griepentrog and Pauline Wilde Richards

©2007 Linda Turner Griepentrog and Pauline Wilde Richards

Published by

An Imprint of F+W Publications

700 East State Street • Iola, WI 54990-0001
715-445-2214 • 888-457-2873
www.krausebooks.com

Our toll-free number to place an order or obtain
a free catalog is (800) 258-0929.

The following registered trademark terms and companies appear in this publication: Angelina®, Aunt Martha's Iron-on Transfers, Baby Lock™, Beacon Adhesives, Bernina™, Brother®, Bubblewrap™, Caron®, Clover Needlecraft, Coats & Clark, Colonial Needle, Colonial Patterns, Crafter's Pick™, Dancing Needleworks, Disney™, DMC™, Embellisher™, Fab Felter™, Fabri-Solvy™, Fabri-Tac™, Fanatica Fibers, Feltcrafts™, Fusible Warm Fleece, Husqvarna® Viking®, Jacquard Products, Janome™, June Tailor®, Kandi™ Corp., Kandi Kane™, Klaer International, KK2000™, Lion Brand Yarns, Lumiere®, MacPhee™ Workshop, Mickey Mouse™, Mix 'n Match Templates for Quilters™, My Favorite Thimble, Mylar™, National Nonwovens™, Plaid®, Poly-Fil®, Red Heart®, Sewing with Nancy®, ShadedWisps™, Simply® Stencils, Soy Silk®, Steam-A-Seam2®, Stitch N Shape®, Sulky™ of America, Swarovski®, Tear-Easy®, The Ultimate!® Glue, The Warm™ Company, Ultra-Fine Threader™, Warm & Natural™, WizPick, Woolcombs WoolWisps™, WoolFelt™, Xpression

Library of Congress Catalog Number: 2006935659

ISBN: 978-0-89689-485-3

Designed by Heidi Bittner-Zastrow
Edited by Tracy L. Conradt

Printed in United States of America

Cover photos
Machine: Courtesy of Bernina of America, Inc.
Felting tool: Courtesy of My Favorite Thimble

Acknowledgments

We would like to thank several people for their help with this book, not only in providing products for us to use, but also for providing inspiration and sharing their own fiber creations for us to share with you. Look for the names of talent fiber artists throughout the text and the gallery sections.

Special thanks go to Janet Klaer, who sent us a large box of fabric from her well-organized stash, so that we could felt it up for projects in the book. Keep in mind that we also had lots of fabric of our own, but the grass is always greener elsewhere, and that's true with fabrics as well.

Kudos to artist Missy Shepler for drawing our how-tos. Because she's a sewer and fiber artist herself, she has understanding of what she's trying to communicate through her illustrations, making it easier for you to visualize the project steps.

Thanks go as well to our industry friends who supplied us with ideas and contacts of notable felters so that we could share their work with you.

And many thanks to our husbands, Keith and John, who put up with our fabric and fiber madness on a daily basis...we love what we do and appreciate their support.

Contents

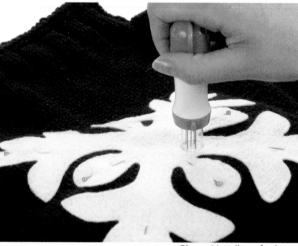

Clover Needlecraft photo

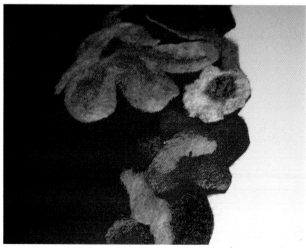

Bernina of America photo

Projects

Introduction

Who would have thought I'd be writing about needle felting? I've always shied away from anything related to handwork, and zealously pursued challenging the sewing machine with unusual tasks. I'd always opt to do anything by machine that I could.

Then, one day I was introduced to the Baby Lock Embellisher, a machine dedicated to felting. An astute salesperson was armed with some wonderful woolly samples that got me hooked on the potential. After all, I love anything related to fibers and fabric.

As a weaver many years ago, the lure of fabulous fibers was simmering again and the creative potential with this specialty machine seemed unrivaled.

I was hooked, and began researching the topic, only to find other machine options available, and a huge following of those who needle felt by hand, doing some things not possible by machine. Hmmm...sign me up and let me at the tools and fibers. I started wondering, as I often do, "I wonder if you could..." You will find the answers to many of those speculations in this book, as most visions I had for creative options worked out.

My good friend, and now co-author, Pauline Richards immediately took to the machine as well and was equally leery of the hand option, but lo and behold, she now loves it, too. It seems each method has its purpose. Both of us have been strong advocates for machine work in our sewing writing careers, but as we've discovered with needle felting, handwork does have its place.

Our approach to needle felting is that it's great fun and that's what should be explored. We have included some technical information in the book as well, just so you know the facts about what could easily become your latest creative addiction.

So, join us in this wonderful, woolly adventure and felt your heart out creating some easy-to-learn projects we've developed to help you explore a variety of techniques. Grab the fibers, and let the barbs begin (on the needles, that is).

~ Linda

There's something very soothing about working with fabric, fibers or yarns and for me, needle felting by hand or machine is wonderful therapy because it brings these three elements together in a unique way. Needle felting has opened a new avenue for self-expression.

I always enjoy visiting fabric or yarn shops even when I don't have a project in mind. I love to look for inspiration and enjoy spending time "feeling" the fibers. Needle felting allows me to build, layer, coax, combine and create using all parts of my abundant fiber stash.

What could be better than co-authoring a book on a technique I love, with my friend and mentor, Linda Griepentrog. Together we see unending possibilities to combine needle felting with many other creative techniques. This book is just the beginning of our ideas and it's a privilege to share our creative journey with you.

Let the felting begin!

~ Pauline

Warning!

Needle felting can be very addicting, so plan storage space for the fibers, fabrics and tools you'll accumulate.

CHAPTER 1
What's all the fuzz about?

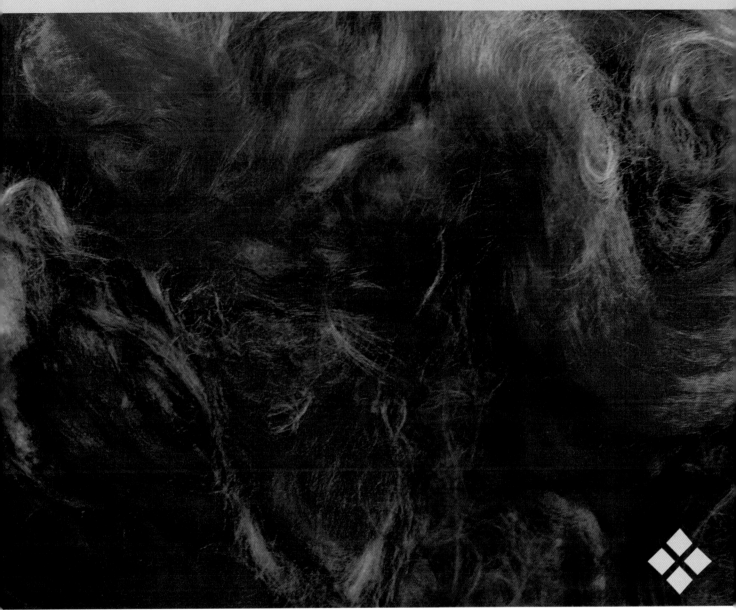

Conjoined Creations Soy Silk photo

There's a buzz about needle felting that creative people can't ignore.

Colorful, fuzzy fibers lure us into the "have-to-do-it" mode,

but how did it all start?

A Bit of History

We can probably blame the first remnants (no pun intended) of felting on the cavemen who used sheepskins to protect their bodies and feet from the weather. Add in precipitation and the friction of walking around in the wild in their daily pursuit of prey, and you have the first stages of the felting frenzy.

Felt can be created by two processes: dry felting and wet felting, and our cavemen utilized the second for their wardrobing.

When water is added to wool fiber, it raises the scales. When accompanied by friction and heat, the fibers interlock to form a dense mass and felting results. In the case of our early ancestors, the felting process was likely accidental. As they stomped around in the wild and laundered their clothes on wet stones, fibers of their wooly body coverings matted and shrunk, creating primitive felt.

Perhaps you too have accidentally created felt—pulling your previously size large wool sweater from the dryer now ready to fit your youngest child! The fibers seem compacted and the texture has changed from soft and cuddly to strangely stiff and inflexible, the neck hole now lucky to fit your wrist.

Both the caveman's felting and the unintended shrinking of a favorite wool sweater illustrate the concept of wet felting.

Dry Felting

Needle felting, a dry-felting technique, is a method of using barbed needles, not moisture and agitation, to entangle fibers either with other like fibers forming dimensional pieces, or into a base fabric creating flat felting.

Barbed needle machines were first created in the late 1800s to make insulation and battings from recycled materials like old shredded woolen garments, animal hair, etc. The needle barbs grab fiber on the downward punch and with repeated stabs, the fibers are locked together creating felted materials.

Today dry felting can be done by hand using single or multiple-needle tools, or by machines using multiple needles for the punching process.

Dry felting techniques are the focus of this book, though they may be combined with wet felting methods as well, and you will see just a few of those pieces in the book.

Before we get into more technical information about needle felting, there are some terms to understand that will be used in the following technique and project chapters, so perk up those memory cells and take note.

Felt Fluency

Below are listed some common terms used in needle felting. Note that they will be expanded upon in subsequent chapters, so only brief definitions are included here.

Barbs
Minute projections on the shaft of a felting needle that actually catch and push the fibers into other fibers and intertwine them for structure.

Base
Fabric or fibers to which other fibers are interlocked to create felt.

Blending
Combining two or more fibers together to take advantage of the best qualities of each. For example, silk is often combined with wool for greater sheen. Since silk fibers do not have the scales of wool for interlocking with other fibers, the two fibers complement each other.

Crimp

The natural dimension of a wool fiber, creating a microscopic appearance of a coiled spring or wavy pasta.

Dry felting

Using repetitive motion and a barbed needle to join fibers. As the name suggests, no moisture is used in the felt creation process.

Gauge

The size (diameter) of a felting needle.

Wool Crimp

Feathering

The process of using untwisted yarn or roving to thinly disperse fibers onto the base fabric creating a wispy look, less dense than felting an entire twist of the same yarn.

Fiber

Any yarn, fabric, roving or other strands used for the felt-making process. Wool is the best fiber to use, but silk, rayon, soy and metallic fibers can also be used in conjunction with the wool.

Mat

A protective layer or surface placed under the base fabric into which the barbed needle stabs. In addition to dense foam, a stiff brush may be used to protect the surface (or fingers) during the felting process.

Punching (stabbing)

The repetitive process of stabbing fibers into a base fabric or into other fibers.

Roving

Slubby yarn

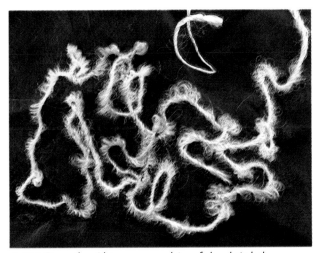
Artist Dorothy Akiyama machine felted tightly twisted yarns (at the upper edge) and they opened up to become loopy.

Roving

Untwisted fibers that form the basis (when twisted) of yarn. Roving fibers are combed or carded so that the fibers lie parallel and look like a rope. The fibers are cleaned and sometimes blended with other colors or fibers. Roving can be purchased by colors groupings, by the pound or by the length.

Scales

The minute projections on the wool fiber shaft that allow it to be interlocked with other fibers or fabrics. These scales are also called corticles and mimic those found on human hair.

Slubs

Slubs are uneven portions of yarn created during the spinning process. The term can also refer to a knot. Although slubs can be indicators of poor quality yarn or an inexperienced spinner, more often they are created purposefully to create interest in the yarn. Slubby yarns are sometimes referred to as "thick and thin," which indicates their character.

Twisting

The yarn-making process that tightens fibers together in the spinning process. Yarns can be twisted tightly or loosely, evenly twisted or slubby (unevenly twisted).

Wet felting

A combination of moisture, heat and pressure applied to fibers (usually wool), causing them to meld together without weaving or knitting.

Wool

Most commonly, wool is hair from a sheep, but hair from camels, alpacas, angora or cashmere goats, llama and vicuna is often referred to with the generic wool designation.

CHAPTER 2
High-Fiber Options

Lion Brand Yarns

Who isn't captivated by fabulous fibers?

Wonderful colors, a soft feel and a vision for their use

can overwhelm us the minute we see them.

Fiber Facts

Several different fibers can be used for the needle-felting process, either in their unspun state as simple loose fibers, in their combed state as roving, or twisted into yarns (which needle felters often untwist!).

Natural Fibers

Wool

Wool is the fiber of choice for needle felting, as the structure of the fiber makes it the ideal choice to meld with others for fabulous creations.

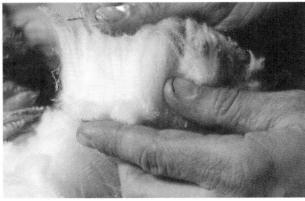

American Sheep Industry photo

By nature, wool fibers are three-dimensional. They have a crimped structure allowing them to stretch up to 30% when dry (and 50% when wet).

American Sheep Industry photo

The shaft of wool fibers is covered with corticles or scales which help it to interlock with other fibers.

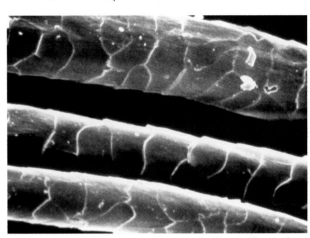

American Sheep Industry photo

Wool fiber quality varies depending on location of the hair on the animal, cleaning and processing of the fibers, but more importantly, the actual length of the fiber. Longer fibers (over 3") are usually deemed higher quality for manufacturing fabrics, and there is less tendency for the finished fabric to pill. The same holds true for needle felting. Longer fibers wear better for yarns and roving used in projects. Shorter fibers and lesser quality yarns may pill or pull apart with age.

When purchasing wool yarns, consider those packaged for needlepoint and other stitchery uses, as the quantity of yarn is smaller than when buying skeins for knitting. Readily available wool such as Merino, Corriedale and Shetland work well for felting. These fibers can be found at most stores which carry wool products.

Mohair

Angora Goat

Mohair fibers come from the angora goat and they are often combined with wool to add sheen and a novelty look to the work. Mohair tops can be quite curly and add lots of texture to a felted piece.

Mohair fibers are fine and long (4" to 12"), white, strong and lustrous. They take dye well like their wool counterparts, although there are also colored angora goats whose fleece is used as is without dyeing. The fibers are generally expensive, which is a practical reason to meld them with other less-expensive animal hairs.

Angora

Angora rabbit, Buttercup; owner/breeder, Margaret Bartold

This category of fibers is often confusing, as there are both angora goats and angora rabbits. The angora goat produces mohair fiber, so the other fiber is technically referred to as angora rabbit hair.

Angora rabbit hair fibers are long and usually white, though sometimes bordering on gray. The fibers are extremely lightweight and are always blended with other fibers, such as wool or rayon, for any needlework use. Angora rabbit hair will not felt on its own.

Camel fibers

A grouping of several related animals—camel, llama, alpaca and vicuna—produce novelty fibers

that are sometimes referred to as wool, but in a scientific sense they aren't actually wool.

Though luxurious and usually expensive, these fibers can be

Llama

combined with wool for textural accents. The camel fibers do have a scaled structure like wool and are most commonly used in their natural colors.

Alpaca

Silk

Silk fibers are produced by silk worms, not from a hair source like the wool and mohair fibers. The silk filaments are relatively smooth once the natural seracin (silk glue) is removed during processing.

Silk fibers are lustrous and can be blended with wool to add sheen to a needle-felted project. Silk bits are often added to roving and yarn for textural interest, as they give it a nubby appearance.

Soy Silk

One of the newest fibers on the market, Soy Silk yarns are a byproduct of the tofu manufacturing process. The soy proteins and liquid are cooked, then extruded (envision pouring water through a colander) through tiny holes to create continuous yarns. Although they look like silk, soy fibers are often called "vegetable cashmere" as they offer the same hand as animal cashmere—soft and silky. Some soy fibers reflect light and look like silk, hence the brand name Soy Silk.

Soy fibers need to be combined with wool for felting, as the fibers have no scales of their own to interlock with a fabric base.

Silk Worms   *Cristoph Fritzsch photo*

Soy Silk

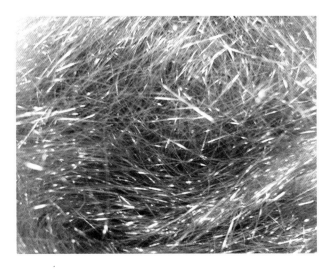

Man-Made Fibers

Angelina

A light-reflective synthetic fiber, this wonderful additive to needle felting adds sparkle and almost a metallic look. The thin fibers will not felt on their own, but they can be combined with other feltable fibers as accents. Some Angelina fibers are heat sensitive and can actually be bonded to each other to form a sheet of fiber that can be incorporated into felted projects. One type of Angelina fiber has a heat-set crimp that mimics the texture of wool fibers.

Metallics

Unto themselves, metallic fibers do not felt, but they can be successfully combined with wool to add sparkle and shine to a needle-felted project. Metallic yarns and threads can be flat, foil structure or twisted fibers, depending on their construction. Some metallics are fragile and may break or split during the punching process, so care is needed to preserve them. Large quantities should be avoided, but they can be used sparingly as accents or for focal point felting areas (like flower centers) in tandem with wools.

Synthetics

Man-made fibers such as polyester, nylon, acrylic, etc. are filament yarns, meaning that they are extruded from a liquid source. (See Soy Silk fibers.) Though they may be treated to add texture, the filaments do not have the scales found in wool fibers and thus they will not work for felting on their own. They can, however, be readily combined with wool for special effects, texture and interest in needle-felted pieces.

Many companies sell yarn samplers offering short lengths of several types of yarns. For felting fun, play with various types of yarns and see what works best (and what doesn't).

Fabrics

In addition to felting the fibers previously mentioned, needle felting can be done using already made fabrics. Wool, boiled wool, wool felt (or blends with some synthetic fibers) and sweater fabric are common choices, and precut shapes, like leaves or flower petals, are often felted to wool base.

For novelty looks, try organdy, organza, netting and other novelties, keeping in mind they might need to be complemented with more feltable fibers for stability.

Because they are not loose fibers, fabric pieces may need some extra punching to hold into the base, and often iron-on interfacing is used on the wrong side to ensure security comparable to a fibrous beginning. Apply fusible interfacing after the felting is completed.

When felting fabric, keep in mind that the two sides will look very different from each other, so decide which you prefer before beginning the felting process.

Wet-felted fabrics and sweaters are a great base for needle felting, as their fibers are compact and dense, holding the embellishment fibers in place securely.

Sometimes needle felting is complete and then the project is actually wet felted, locking in the fibers and shrinking the fabric and/or design prior to construction. For more on this technique, see Knit Wits on page 83.

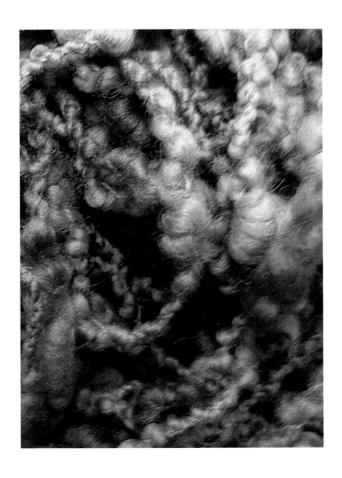

Not Your Ordinary Felting

Designer Dorothy Akiyama loves to play with yarns, fibers and fabrics. As an avid knitter and fiber artist, there's nothing that she won't try! Below are some of her needle felting samples on non-traditional fabrics.

Novelty yarns blend well with discharged fabric (color altered).

Silk organza makes the perfect base for twisted yarns.

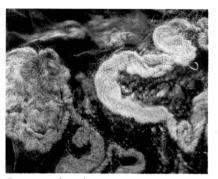

Rayon velvet becomes even more sumptuous with felted yarn work.

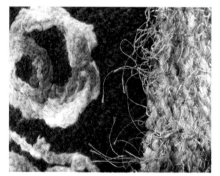

Knitted yardage accents similar color yarn felted shapes.

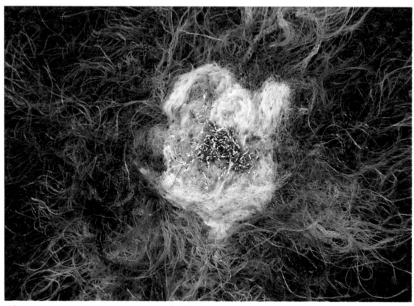

Shaggy yarns create a beautiful felted fuzz.

Metallic yarn accents a print fabric base.

CHAPTER 3

Tools of the Trade

Unlike many other hobbies, needle felting requires minimal investment in tools to begin, but that's quickly made up for as you develop a passion for fibers! As indicated in the book title, needle felting can be done by hand or machine, and in some instances, by both within the same piece. For more information on machine felting, see Ready, Set, Felt by Machine on page 43.

Hand Felting Needles

Single Needles

Felting can be done with a single needle in areas of fine detail, like the corners of our On the Flip Side bag on page 73. Single-needle felting is also done on three-dimensional pieces where the felting process is used to create intricate features on gnomes, fairies, ornaments, etc.

Single needles come with a bent handle for better grip than just a straight-needle shaft. Some also come with coated handles for a better grip, or the needle may have a wooden handle for easier manipulation.

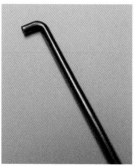

For single needles without any handle gripper, needle felters often wrap the upper bent portion with a rubber band for better gripping.

Because the needles are barbed, they can be very dangerous, so care should be taken to store needles properly to prevent damage and injury. Several companies sell tubes and cases for safe storage, or you can use a straw or coffee stirrer to protect the barbed shaft.

Some felters like to store the needles they're working with along the edges of their foam base, along with large pins used for positioning yarn. Always dispose of bent or broken needles safely by wrapping before discarding them in the trash.

If you plan to teach children to needle felt, be sure they understand how dangerous the barbed needles can be and that they must be treated with care to prevent injury.

Multiple-Needle Tools

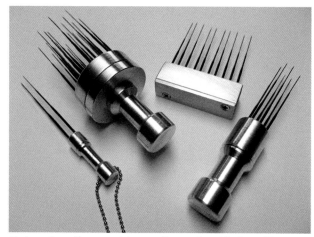

Feltcrafts offers multi-needle tools with 2 to 20 needle options.

The felting process goes faster with multiple needles, as opposed to a single needle, if the space and design allow for it. Several companies make felting tools in various configurations and with different numbers and sizes of needles, from 2 to 25! Color code the top of your needles by size for quick reference.

Some tools have wooden handles, others have plastic (rigid or flexible) handles, and still others have metal handles, all for easy gripping. Most multi-needle tools arrange the needles in a circular formation, but a few offer a linear arrangement similar to a comb.

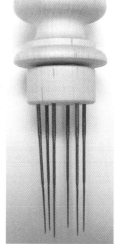

The round wooden screw-off handle on this Colonial Needle tool allows for a sturdy hold and easy replacement of needles.

My Favorite Thimble photo

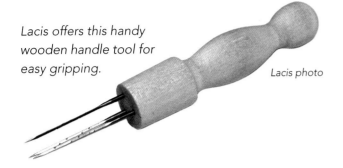

Lacis offers this handy wooden handle tool for easy gripping.

Lacis photo

Clover Needlecraft offers a spring-loaded plastic tool holding five needles. The needles are surrounded with a protective shield, which retracts with each stab of the tool. Not only does this protect fingers against exposed needles, but it also allows for consistent penetration depth. The tool locks to protect needles during transport. Needles can be removed for detail work, and broken needles can be replaced individually if they bend or break. This tool works well for children.

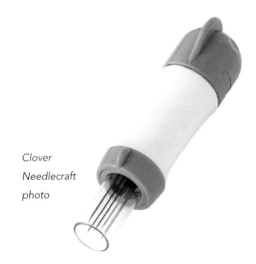

Clover Needlecraft photo

Whatever tool you choose, be sure that needles can be replaced. Most tools use an Allen wrench or a Phillip's head screw driver to disassemble the tool; a few require unscrewing a portion of the handle to re-insert needles. Some multi-needle tools do not allow you to replace needles at all and you simply use fewer needles when one breaks, or dispose of the tool completely.

What a treat!

If you're looking for something special for your gift list, visit www.Woolcombs.com. Andrew Forsyth hand turns exotic hardwoods to create elegant handles for felting tools. Shapes vary from mushroom (short and round) to this long penlike "Elegant Felter," and the removable head can hold from one to five needles at a time in any configuration you prefer.

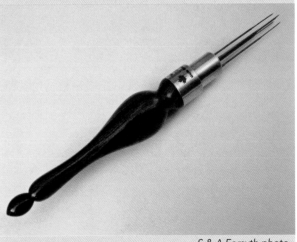

S & A Forsyth photo

Needle Gauge & Shapes

Felting needles are 3" to 3½" long and have an upside down L shape. The hook on the top is the handle when using a single needle, or it fits into some type of handle for multi-needle tools or for easier handling of a single needle.

The needle shaft is covered with barbs or indentations, which interlock the fibers during the felting process. The number of barbs and the location on the needle shaft vary.

Felting needle shafts can be triangular or star shape and the more surfaces with barbs, the faster the needle felting process. Star shaped needles have more barbs than triangular needles as they have an extra surface.

The size of the needle diameter is referred to as the gauge. Common sizes include 32 to 42. The higher the number, the thinner the needle shaft. When purchasing needles, sometimes the actual gauge isn't listed; they are only referred to as "coarse" or "fine." A size 32 needle is used for deep or coarse felting and a size 42 is used for finishing or fine felting.

The size choice depends on the project and the amount of fine detail needed. Many felters have multiple sizes of needles for differing purposes. For example, when laying down fibers initially, a coarser needle works well and then a finer needle can be used for the finishing. For minute faces on dolls or fiber sculptures, the finest needle allows for detailing eyes and facial features like cheeks and lips.

Keep in mind, the thinner the shaft, the more easily the needle can break. An awl or a bamboo skewer works well to push and arrange fibers instead of using your felting needle.

When felting fabric to fabric, finer needles leave fewer visible holes in the fabric, particularly if it's a lightweight or sheer fabric.

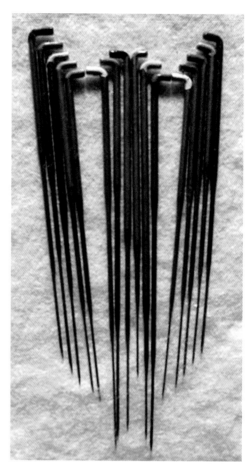

Wizpick photo

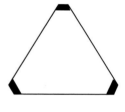

Triangle and star shaped needle shafts have barbs on all sides.

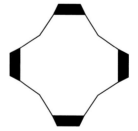

Felting needles are often available in sampler packs, offering multiple sizes and/or shapes. If you only want to purchase one needle type and size, a 38 triangle needle works well for general felting.

A sampler pack allows you to try different sizes and shapes of needles.

Protective Bases

Because of the barbs on the felting needle shaft, some protection is needed for the surface on which you felt, be it the table top, your lap or simply your hand for tiny pieces. The base serves as a receptacle for the repetitive punches of the needle and it must not get caught in the retraction process of each punching motion.

My Favorite Thimble photo

Foam

Very dense foam is frequently used as a protective base for felting, as the barbs of the needle do not get caught in it during the punching process. Over time, the foam will deteriorate from the repeated penetrations, and it's easy and inexpensive to simply purchase a new slab. The size of the foam block depends on the project—a 4" block is common, though many felters prefer a larger or smaller chunk depending on their project. For hand-held felting, a slab that fits in the palm works well to protect the skin below.

Foam comes in various densities and thicknesses, so choose one that feels right to you, or opt for foam bases designed and packaged specifically for needle felters. Do not use floral form as it is not made for felting. Needle felting foam has been infused with plastic to make it extremely sturdy and long lasting.

Other options include denims of all sorts, making needle felting a perfect combo for jean and jacket embellishing. Be sure the denim you're using does not have spandex fibers in it (for stretch), as those elastic fibers can be severely damaged by repeated needle punching.

Nancy's Notions photo

Brush

An inverted brush, similar to a scrub brush, is a relatively recent needle felting introduction by Clover Needlecraft. The brush works best with the Clover felter as other tools or needles can penetrate the brush too far and can break when they hit the base. Like foam, the fabric is placed over the stiff brush and the non-slip base serves as a protector for the table, lap or hand under it.

Brush bases are available in different sizes, depending on the size of the project.

Under it All

Whether you're needle felting by hand or machine, on flat projects you need to have some foundation to felt into. The needle(s) must be able to punch easily into the base without stress, so it's best to avoid very densely constructed materials.

Wool of all types works well and the flexible fibers allow the needles to pass through without strain. Lightweight wools, openwork weaves and a variety of knits all make wonderful substrates. Boiled wool and felted wools are also good choices, as is flannel and coat-weights, including melton cloth.

Sweaters beckon needle felted embellishments and the knitted structure makes the process easy. Sweaters that have already been felted themselves are great, too.

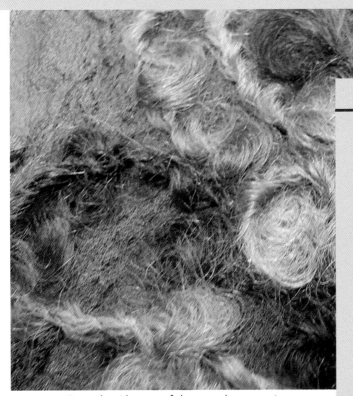

Designer Dorothy Akiyama felts novelty yarns into a lightweight silk base.

Lightweight fabrics like organdy, organza and other sheers have potential to be felted when used as a base fabric, but they may suffer damage from the repeated needle penetrations. This "damage" can also be perceived to be texture by artisans. Test-felt to see how they hold up before basing a project on these lightweights and note that you may need fusible interfacing of some sort behind the felting to hold the fibers in place on anything subjected to wear.

Outerwear fleece also works well as a base, though care must be taken not to stretch the fleece during the felting process.

For home décor and craft items, burlap can also be a functional base. For the more adventurous, lightweight felting can be done on handmade and other sturdy papers. Because paper is delicate you will not be able to felt the paper as you would fabric.

Tapestries and upholstery-weight fabrics are also workable, and the fabric patterning may be used to fill in with fibers. For more on this technique, see Coloring Inside the Lines on page 93.

Melton Feltin'

One of our favorite fabrics for a needle felting base is melton cloth, a tightly woven wool with a short nap. It comes in some great colors and works fabulously for vests, coats, jackets and even small projects and accessories. Because it's very compactly woven, the edges can be left raw or trimmed with decorative scissors or rotary cutter blades.

Another favorite base is wool coating or duffle, not as compact as melton, it's slightly fuzzy making it a great match with wool roving and yarns.

A great source for both melton and duffle coatings in many colors is MacPhee Workshop. See the Resource listing on page 125 for contact information.

Placement Points

Placing and holding yarns and fibers on the fabric for the felting process can be tricky, especially for synthetics that don't "grip" the surface. A stiletto, bamboo skewer or a single felting needle can be used to shape and position the fibers exactly where you want them when felting by hand or machine.

Design Wise

Where will you get your ideas and patterns for needle felting? Simply, everywhere! Look around you for flowers in your garden, photos of favorite places, pets and landscaping. If none of those inspire you, look to other designers for help.

Patterns and Kits

Needle-felting patterns and kits are available from several sources. We've listed many resources in the back of the book to guide you to some companies with supplies.

As with all creative endeavors, it's important not to violate copyright law. You cannot just copy someone's designs and use them for your own purposes without permission.

There are many sources of copyright-free artwork—from books and Internet sites, to CDs and leaflets. Be sure to read the fine print for any limitations on use, particularly if you plan to sell your finished pieces. If you're in doubt about whether or not you can use any artwork, ask!

Quilt patterns, coloring books and appliqué patterns can also provide inspiration for fabulous felting. Some patterns also come pre-printed on fabric, designed for other needlework techniques but adaptable to needle felting.

Embroidery Patterns

Hand embroidery patterns or digitized machine embroidery motifs can be used as patterns for felting. Inside details may be left off and just the outlined portion used for filled-in areas, or details may be used as guidelines for highlighting the felting with beads or fine-line yarnwork.

Iron-on transfers designed for hand embroidery and Redwork also work well for felting patterns. Follow the directions to iron the design to the base fabric.

Stencils and Templates

Stencils can also be used for needle felting pattern making. Simply trace the design onto the base fabric using a removable marker or chalk. Ideally, the markings will be covered by the felting fibers, but in the event that they are not, it's good to be able to remove them. Air-soluble markers and disappearing chalks work well for marking on most fabrics; water-removable markers are suitable only for fabrics not damaged by the water used for the removal process.

Plaid Simply Stencils, #28986

June Tailor Mix 'n Match Templates for Quilters come in multiple sizes in the same shape.

Stencils can also be used in combination with a temporary spray adhesive and left in place for the felting process as you fill the design area. Simply spray the underside of the stencil and press it in place on the fabric surface. Felt within the outlined area. Note that to prevent damage to the stencil, it's best to do this with hand felting needles. If you're using the machine or a multi-needle tool for felting, outline the shape with a single needle first, then remove the stencil before filling in the area to protect the stencil from errant punctures.

Quilt and appliqué templates can also be used to make felting patterns. Trace around the motif edge and remove the pattern.

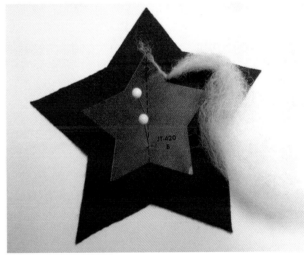

Needle felting can be done on the template outline or outside pattern lines, depending on the desired look, and the same stencil or template can produce two different looks. For a third, fill in the shape!

Free-Form Felting

Keep in mind that many needle felting creations can be done without any clearly defined plan—free-form design can "just happen" as you let the fibers and fabrics speak to you! These abstract arrangements are great fun to create and a good way to practice needle felting techniques. They're useful for small projects like pin cushions, purse flaps, collars, cuffs, etc. or they can be framed as art on their own.

Fabric Patterning

Although printed fabric designs are copyrighted, you can use them for inspiration for needle felted designs. For example, make a printed fabric skirt to go with a jacket that you felt with a similar looking motif. For more information on this technique, see Flower Power on page 97.

Designer Kathy McMannis used free-form yarnwork to fill in this jean jacket design and create the coordinating purse.

Brother International photo

CHAPTER 4
Super Starters

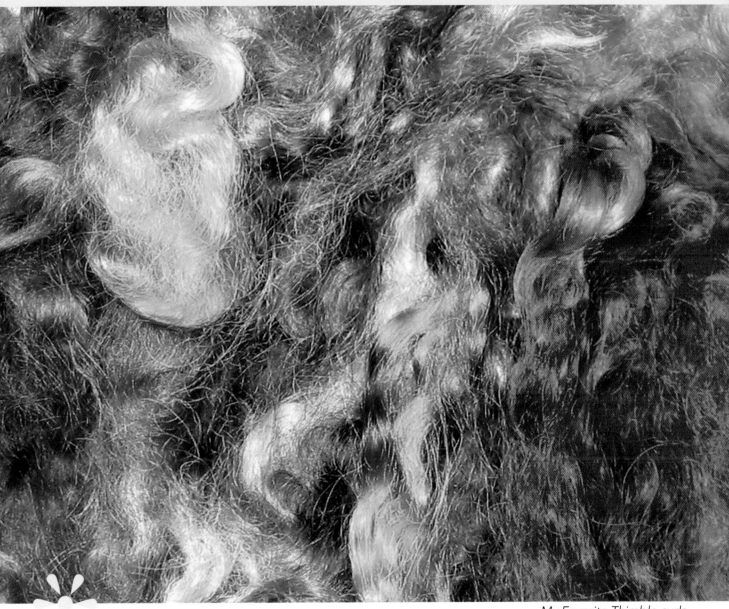

My Favorite Thimble curls

Needle felting can be done either by hand or by machine,

or a combination of both. Preparation is the same for both venues

and is key to the success of your project.

The Choice is Yours

Although needle felting works equally well by hand or by machine in most instances, there are advantages to each process. The choice you make will depend on the project and the investment you want to make, as well as available space in your sewing room.

Hand needle felting requires relatively little out-lay in equipment. You need only a needle and fiber for the simplest operation, and for even the most complex creations, add to that a piece of foam or brush protector mat under your work and perhaps a multi-needle tool. Hand felting is a very portable activity if you have time to pass while traveling or at family events, or just need a TV activity.

Hand felting allows you to create three-dimensional objects, like dolls, figurines, ornaments, Easter eggs, etc. that are impossible to create using a machine. Needle sizes can be varied depending on the amount of detail needled, and multi-needle tools can be used for greater coverage area with each punch.

Needle felting by hand also allows you to access areas you might not be able to reach by machine without "reverse sewing" something. For example, when felting by hand, you can punch motifs onto a narrow sleeve or pant leg. In addition, hand needle felting allows you to pinch and shape surrounding areas while felting, like when detailing doll faces to fashion chins, cheeks and furrowed brows.

On the other hand (no pun intended) to felt by machine, you can spend from $300 to more than $1,000 for a dedicated machine, or less for an attachment to an existing machine if one is available for your particular model. In addition, you need space to put the dedicated machine if you plan to use it regularly.

Machine felting is limited to flat pieces, and you can cover a large space with great speed and very consistent penetration of the barbed needles. Some machines allow for the removal of needles to allow for finer detailing, others require the use of all needles at all times. Machine felting helps to anchor non-feltable fibers better than hand felting, as its repeated strong penetrations push fibers into the base.

Both methods require fiber and/or fabric, and of course you need a multitude of colors and "must-have" textures to work with.

Taking Care

As you're planning your needle felting project, think about how the final item will be cared for. Will it be washed, dry cleaned or simply brushed off?

Felted items that will be washed may take on a totally different look after being subjected to water and agitation. Both the base fabric and the fibers may shrink, depending on the fiber content. In other instances, only one of those may shrink, leading to some interesting results!

It's best to dry clean your felted projects to maintain their original look, unless you're purposefully planning for shrinkage and wet felting as part of the finished look.

For wall hangings and home décor items, a gentle vacuuming or dusting may be the only care needed.

1-2-3 Go!

Needle felting is an easy activity to become involved in. No long-term training is required and you just need to have a sense of adventure and a "can-do" attitude. Respect the barbs on the needles and realize that they can be dangerous if used incorrectly.

We suggest that you gather some scraps and practice and play with the techniques we've outlined in the next chapter before you start to work on an actual project. Keep samples and label them with the fiber or yarn and base fabric information for future reference. If you have different sizes and shapes of needles, note what was used on each sample as well.

Designer Melissa Brown tried felting with several types of fabrics and fibers on a sampler sheet.

Windows of the World

Capture one fabric, perhaps a non-feltable, between two layers of feltable fabrics— one with cut-out shapes so the oddity can peek through. Melissa Brown framed some colorful cottons using this technique, but also think about family photos printed on fabric or bold graphics peering out from under the upper felted fabric.

Pattern Planning

If your project requires a specific design, draw the pattern on the right side of the fabric using chalk or a disappearing marker, depending on the base color. The goal is to cover the lines with the fibers as they're secured, but it's good to have a back-up plan for removal if some lines show.

To use an iron-on transfer, follow the manufacturer's instructions for applying it to the right side of the base fabric.

For garment or project sections (like collars, cuffs, etc.) where a specific size and shape are needed, outline the shape on the fabric right side, but keep in mind that this should be only a guideline. As you felt there will be some take-up, or shrinkage, in both the fibers and the fabric, so it's best to cut the base larger than needed by a few inches each direction and trim it to size later.

Allow extra length for fiber take-up as well, as with each needle penetration some length is lost, particularly in densely felted areas.

Remember that needle felting has no right or wrong side, so determine from your sample which one you want to be the outside of your work, depending on the look you like—clear and crisp, or more muted.

Right Side, Wrong Side

Take a look at the right side and wrong side of several of our needle felting samples to see which effect you like best.

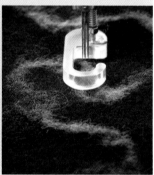

Bernina of America photos

Clover Needlecraft photos

This yarn yields all these individual colors to work with in a project..

The Layout

Choose fibers that are compatible with each other and if you want to use some that won't felt on their own, pair them up with those that felt well. Fibers can be twisted together or used for layering on top of each other for firm holding power.

Lay out all the fibers you've chosen for the project and take a look at the overall appearance to be sure they work well together visually. Note which ones need mates to ensure the felting process is successful.

If you're using yarn, you may want to untwist all or part of it to a fibrous state. For loose fibers, you may want to twist some strands together or separate them for a light, wispy covering only.

Variegated yarns provide a multitude of colors in one strand–separate them as needed for individual hues and textures. Learn to work with your fibers for more versatility.

CHAPTER 5
Fiber + Fabric + Needle = Felting Fun!

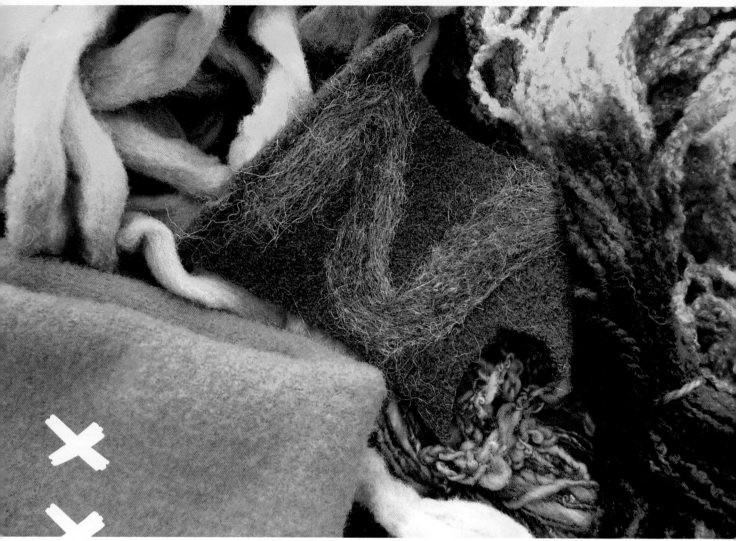

Spinning Ewe fibers

Once you've planned your project and played with the fiber options,

it's time to begin the felting process. Making a sample on the same fabric

as your project using various techniques ensures the look you like.

Needle Up

The felting process involves repeatedly punching fibers into the fabric base using a straight up and down motion. If you stab at an angle, there is a much greater chance for needle breakage. To use a multi-needle tool, hold the tool firmly when punching. Push down and pull up in a repetitive motion using a consistent speed to cover the area you're felting.

Clover Needlecraft photo

Blending colors and twisting yarns add interest and a touch of realism to your needle felting work.

Start your project by "basting" fibers in place, punching only lightly to hold them while you survey the progress. If you like what you see developing, punch more securely to anchor the fibers into the base. To completely felt, the fibers shouldn't easily be pulled out of the base.

Remember, if you create something you're not happy with, just pull out the fibers and start again.

Tip

Synthetics—both fabrics and fibers—are harder on needles than natural fibers and they will dull the points. There is also more chance of needle breakage.

Always begin with the lowermost level of the design and work toward the top. For example, a flower stem and leaves should be done before felting the blossoms.

Fiber colors can be blended as you work, or they can be twisted together as you punch if you didn't do it before you began the felting process. It's best to work in layers rather than trying to felt thick layers at a single pass—and it's easier on the needles and your hands.

Oops!

Felting needles are thin and brittle, and further weakened by the barbs cut into the shaft diameter, so be sure to use only a straight up-and-down motion when felting. Any sideways twisting may snap the needle. When using a multi-needle tool, continue to use the tool with fewer needles if they can't be individually replaced.

Needle Felting Know-How

The following techniques form the basis of most felting projects, either alone or when used together. They can be done by both hand and machine, depending on the project. Practice each separately to get a feel for the felting process.

Meandering

Perhaps the easiest of all needle-felting techniques, meandering yarns are a great place to begin. Simply lay yarn onto the fabric surface and punch it into place. Like all fibers, it's best to lightly stab them in to place first as a "basting," then go back and felt them seriously into place.

Yarns can be looped, zigzagged or simply used to create more controlled outline shapes. If the yarn ends will not be encased in a seamline later, place them under an overlapping yarn to hide them once they're felted into place.

Or, untwist the yarns and felt the ends in a more spread out pattern (feathering) than the rest of the fiber length.

Meandering can be done with almost any trim, yarn or fibers, depending on the desired look. It can also be done on top of lighter felted fibers creating surface interest over background felting.

Pillows make the perfect practice project to try out different felting techniques.

Let yarns extend beyond the edge for a bit of fun.

Outlines

Instead of letting fibers and yarns meander on the fabric surface, outlining channels those strands into controlled shapes, like flowers, leaves, etc.

Outline patterns can be transferred to the fabric using chalk or removable marker, and you simply punch the fibers along the line. Or, you can use outlining to complement a shape already filled in with other fibers, beading, stitchery, etc.

Outlining alone is a quick and easy way to add color to a fabric, without adding any additional bulk from more densely punched fibers.

Coils

Perfect for flower centers, allover circles, lollipops or car wheels, the coiling technique is easy to do and the rings can be made any size, depending on the piece.

Simply coil yarn or fibers in a circular pattern. If the yarn doesn't want to stay in the circle, use a few pins until you have it basted in place with a felting needle.

Coiling is often worked over a previously felted area, like a gauze background or outlined flower petals.

Tuck the end of the wrapped fibers under the last round, or just felt them into the fabric base to finish. For a fun touch, leave the coil ends hanging loose.

Fill-in

Covering the fabric background with fiber can produce some wonderful needle-felted designs and everything from simple to elaborate shapes can be easily filled with colorful yarns or fibers.

While free-form fill-in motifs are possible, most felters like to draw a pattern onto the fabric before picking up their needles. This can be done using a removable marker, chalk or using a stencil while needle felting to maintain the shape.

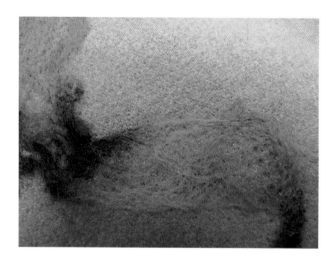

Fill-in can be done prior to or after any outlining, as it forms the design base, accented by other techniques. Areas can be filled in totally with a heavy coverage of fiber, or they can be more lightly filled, allowing some of the background fabric to show through. Use a single hand felting needle to create precise corners and edges with yarn or roving.

Gauze

Pulling apart fibers into thin sheets and needle felting them to the fabric surface produces light, airy sections of color and texture. Gauze can be used as a fill-in technique, making shaped areas, or it can be used overall with other techniques felted on top.

The key to a gauzy look is that fibers are pulled thinly so that they produce very light coverage of the area before they are felted into place. More than one color of fibers can be used together to give a heathery appearance without distinct color breaks.

Feathering

Individual strands of yarn or fiber lengths can be opened up to create a flared section of visually lighter coverage. Used to create flower blossoms and leaves, the technique is also a clever way to finish the work when fiber ends aren't included in a seamline.

Different color fibers can be blended to create more interest as they're opened up.

Bernina of America photo

Designer Nina McVeigh used feathering to create some wispy flower petals.

Tufts

Short, cut fiber or yarn lengths can be felted in place in only one area, leaving the ends free. Tufting can be used to produce texture and dimension in a design.

While most often, the bits are felted at the center, they can also be held in place by needle felting only one end.

Cut your own yarn lengths, or start with pre-cut yarns made for latch hooking–they're all the same length and ready to use.

Tufting is perfect for allover patterning, or it can be used to highlight a single design area. Think about using the technique for animal fur, beards, doll hair, etc.

Faux Stitching

Using simply a single thin yarn strand and a single felting needle, it's easy to mimic the look of hand stitching to accent other needle felting techniques. This "stitching" is much faster than hand sewing running stitches, as it can all be done from the right side.

To create faux stitching, simply needle felt the single strand of yarn in place at regular intervals to mimic handwork. For more complete instructions, see the Autumn Leaves project on page 79.

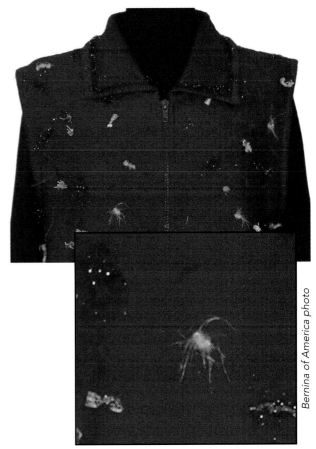

Designer Jo Leichte created this Confetti Vest with tufts of yarns.

Loops

Who said that yarn and fiber had to be needle felted flat onto a fabric base? It's fun to leave loops to create dimensional texture.

To make loops, pull some slack into the length of yarn or fiber and punch in place at regular intervals, creating loops between. The loops can be similar size or vary randomly for more interest; they can be placed sporadically or in regular patterns, depending on the motif. Give them a slight twist for a sure stand-up. This technique requires using a single hand felting needle, as loops are formed individually.

Plaid

Yarns can be worked in grids to imitate plaid. Felt down all one direction first and then the other, or weave them as you go. Draw lines on the fabric surface to help with the spacing and angle, but remember the lines don't have to be spaced evenly.

Raves about Roving

When working with roving, it's helpful to gently twist it slightly as you work. Twisting aligns the fibers and makes it easier to work with. Twirling it a bit also helps eliminate uncontrollable fuzzies and gives your design a more distinct look.

Place the roving into shapes and apply each layer separately. Layer the roving in thin layers, alternating the direction. This will build up color and thickness as needed, as opposed to trying to felt a wad of it at one time.

Same Design, Different Looks

Create a fun sampler and a great reference piece by using coordinating colors and fibers to make a sampler of all the previous mentioned techniques. Pin a tag to each section to refresh your memory about the technique used in a given area.

The same motif can have many, many looks depending on the process and fibers used.

If you're putting together a reference notebook, try felting the same shape or design using a number of the different techniques listed previously. Check out which one you like best and use that one on your actual project.

Felting Fabric

In addition to all the wonderful yarns and fibers on the market to tempt you into oblivion, you can also use fabric for felting. Pre-cut shapes like flowers and leaves give a folkloric appearance when felted to a fabric base. They are especially fun to work with on sweater knit, where the base may have an uneven texture, as the integrity of the fabric gives a smoother appearance.

There are different types and weights of felt on the market, from dense wool felts to thin craft weights, including some with glitter and metallic fibers in them for added sparkle. Thicker felts tend to hold up better to the repeated stabbing of felting needles. Craft-weight felt, such as the 9" x 12" sheets sold in craft stores, can be used for sparser felting but doesn't work as well as 100% wool sheets.

Obviously the best fabrics for felting are wool and wool blends, based on what is known about the fiber's structure. But, you can also use other fabrics for different effects. Organza and lightweight silks are popular options, as are some nettings and textured synthetics.

Clover Needlecraft photo

This machine embroidered lamb is needle felted with short strips of heathery WoolFelt from National Nonwovens. See the lamb pattern on page 100.

Fragile fabrics are best felted minimally to avoid damage as they are easily destroyed by repeated punctures of the barbed needles. Felting with a fine needle and only around the edges will hold them in place, and combining them with more feltable fibers and yarns will anchor them without visible damage.

Know When to Stop

Whether you're felting yarns or fabrics, there is a point where you need to stop. If you overfelt, the fibers will lose their dimension and look flat. Overfelted fabrics will lose their character and the fibers will be damaged by excessive puncturing—unsightly holes may be visible.

When working with pre-cut felt shapes like these from CPE Felt, it's best to felt lightly around the edges with a small needle to keep the integrity of the fabric without visible holes.

When punching felt, be careful not to overwork it, as needle holes may be visible.

CHAPTER 6
Ready, Set...
Felt by Machine!

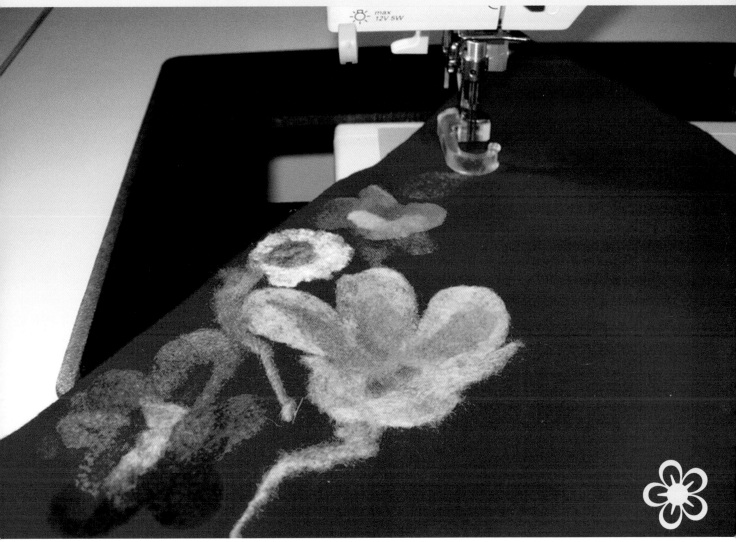

Bernina of America photo

Needle felting by machine is quick and easy

and covers a very large area in a short time.

Invest in a machine or an attachment and felt your heart out.

Machine Magic

Machine felting eliminates the repetitive-motion action of handwork, as the machine does all the work for you. The fiber punching is always a consistent penetration depth, which is not necessarily the case when felting by hand.

Machine work can be used in tandem with hand felting, depending on the project. Large areas can be machine felted, then "detailed" by hand. Or, felt a project by hand and then use the machine to go over it and secure the fibers more than the original hand punching process.

Felting by machine is best for flat projects, not those with dimension, as there is no way to get a 3-D item under the presser foot, so save the fairies and gnomes for hand techniques.

If you're felting with non-feltable fabrics or yarn types, machine felting will punch them deeper and more securely into the base than hand felting.

The Motion Notion

All machine needle felting is done free-motion, meaning that the machine doesn't feed the fabric for you as it does for traditional sewing. There are no feed dogs to ensure consistent stitch length, but with felting you have no stitches and not a strand of thread to worry about. The barbed needles simply go up and down in the needle hole(s), entangling fibers as they go. Because you are responsible for moving the fabric, it may take a bit of adjustment to the free-motion maneuvering if you're not used to that responsibility.

To move the fabric for felting, hold both hands solidly on the fabric in front and to the sides of the foot and move at a smooth, even pace randomly to cover the area.

If you're a quilter used to stippling or a free-motion embroiderer, the movement will come naturally as it's the same process used for those techniques.

The speed at which you run the machine coupled with the fabric movement will determine the amount of felting. If you run the machine slowly and move the fabric freely, you'll be "basting" the components in place. This is a good thing to do so components don't move around as you're designing. But, keep in mind you will need to go back over them to fully felt the fibers in place.

If basting isn't in your designing repertoire and you'd rather "just do it," run the machine at a faster pace securely anchoring the fibers on the first pass. Remember faster is okay but you may have more needle breakage. Since the machine has no thread, there's no worry about stitching off the fibers as you move–simply move the fabric so you're back on them.

Remember, it's easier to remove fibers if you don't like the look if they're only lightly held in place, so "basting" helps you audition the design before finishing.

Some machine companies advise felting the fibers from one side, then felting from the other side, and perhaps even a third time from the original side to securely lock the fibers into the fabric. This decision can be made as you determine the look you like and the type of fibers you're using, as well as the durability needed for the project. Garments with felting done in high-wear areas require more security than a wall hanging.

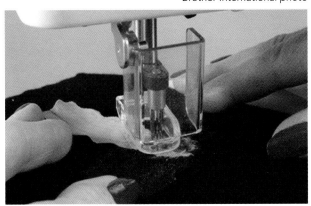

Brother International photo

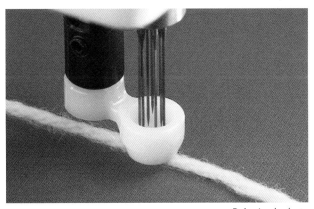

Janome photo

Baby Lock photo

Safeguards

All felting machines have some kind of needle guard to protect your fingers from accidentally being struck by the barbed needles. The guard may be separate from the presser foot, or incorporated into the foot, depending on the brand.

It's best not to disengage or remove the guard, as severe damage can result from the high-speed penetration of barbed needles into your fingers as you guide the work. If you need help shaping yarns and fibers, or holding them in place while you punch, use a stiletto or awl. Pins can also be used, but must be removed before you get to them in the felting process.

When using a machine for felting, it's very important to keep it clean, as the fiber lint builds up rapidly during the felting process. Stopping to clean the machine several times during a large project is advisable for the best performance. Look for a sewing machine brush for this purpose if one is not provided with the machine, or use a tiny vacuum attachment designed for computer cleaning.

To avoid breaking or bending needles while felting, follow these simple tips:

- Practice free-motion stitching on your regular machine to develop a smooth and even rhythm for moving the fabric. Any fast or erratic movements can cause needles to bend or break.

Bernina of America photo

Nancy's Notions photo

- Run the machine at a consistent pace. It's not necessary to slow down or speed up, nor is it necessary to run the machine at its maximum speed, unless that's comfortable for you to control.

- Don't pull or push the fabric while felting. Try not to stop with the needles down in the fabric, as it can be tempting to want a closer look at your work and inadvertently pull on it, bending the needles.

- Don't try to felt something that is too thick to move under the foot. Some presser feet offer height adjustments, but there is a limit to what the needles can go through.

- Be sure to hold the fibers in place as you work so they don't get caught on the presser foot or any thread guides. Hold them outside the needle guard, but as close as possible to keep them in check.

On the Market

There are dedicated machines for felting, or attachments/adapter kits for select models of sewing machines. Before you make a decision, check out all the options to see which best matches your needs. Investigate the configuration and spacing of the needles for the work you plan to do, as the various brands differ in the number of needles, spacing and needle replacement options.

At press time, the following information is accurate, but it's best to check with your local sewing machine dealer for current offerings.

Dedicated Felters
Baby Lock Embellisher

As a dedicated felting machine, the Embellisher holds up to seven needles. An Allen wrench can be used to remove needles if needed for more detailed work, and the machine can be used with a single needle for very fine felting. Needles may be replaced individually if they break.

Baby Lock Embellisher

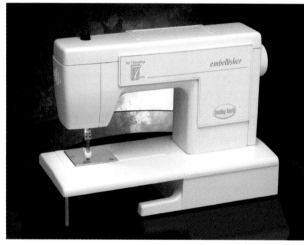

Baby Lock photos

Feltcrafts

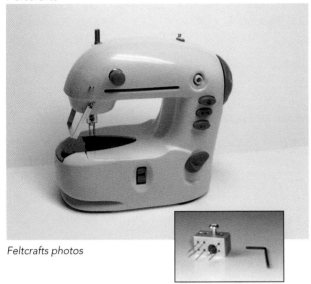

Feltcrafts photos

Conversion Attachment

Huskystar ER10

Husqvarna Viking photo

Janome Xpression

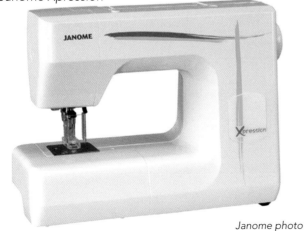

Janome photo

The Embellisher has no feed dogs, no bobbin, no thread and no tension, as you would find on a traditional machine. It does offer a free-arm for access to narrow areas you may want to felt and the presser foot height is adjustable, depending on the thickness of the felting fibers.

Feltcrafts

This specialized company sells a small machine dedicated to felting after conversion from its previous sewing functions. They also have converted some older machines to purely felting functions.

If you have an old sewing machine that you'd like to convert to a felting-only machine, this company sells a multiple-needle adapter for this purpose. Keep in mind, you can't go backward, however–once a felter, always a felter.

Husqvarna Viking Huskystar ER10

With a needle-up stop, this feature makes it easy to remove and manipulate felting projects. The machine features a clear needle guard for finger protection, a slide-out tray to clean fiber and fuzz. The no-tension, no-thread configuration allows for free-motion punching with five individually-replaceable needles. A slide-off table base converts the machine to a free-arm for felting in small areas. The machine also has an adjustable presser bar lever to work with varying thicknesses of felting materials.

Janome Xpression

This dedicated felting machine holds five needles in a single head, and like others, there is no bobbin, no thread, no tension and no feed dogs. In place of a bobbin is a lint catcher to collect extraneous fibers. The free-arm allows access for felting small areas and there's a light for better visibility. The Xpression requires a new needle head (or use with fewer needles) if one or more break.

Pfaff Smart 350p

Five barbed needles, no thread and no tension, coupled with a free-arm convertible base are features of this 6-pound machine. A clear needle guard protects fingers and a convenient lint tray is easy to clean. A slide-out accessory tray adds convenient storage and the machine has a needle-up feature when stopping. An adjustable cloth presser allows for differing material thicknesses. Needles can be replaced separately.

Sewing with Nancy Fab Felter

With five barbed needles, this 12-pound machine is perfect for toting to class or using in your sewing room. There are no feed dogs, no thread, no bobbin and no tension to be concerned with, but there is a handy slide-out dust box to catch all the felting lint. The adjustable needle guard accommodates varying thicknesses of fabrics and fibers. Needles are individually replaceable if they break. A free-arm and lighted sewing area are added benefits.

Conversion Options

When converting any standard sewing machine from its normal function to felting capabilities, be sure to follow the manufacturer's instructions for installation of the conversion components. But, follow these general guidelines:

- The machine must be set for straight stitching, as the multiple felting needles don't allow for any sideways motion.

- Deactivate the feed dogs by lowering or setting the stitch length to zero. All the felting is done with free-motion stitching, so no feed dogs are needed.

- Check to be sure if you need to remove or inactivate other machine functions with the felting set-up. Some machines require removal of the needle threading mechanism.

- Don't forget to lower the presser foot before starting to stitch. It's hard to remember since there is no thread!

- Once you're ready to stitch and all the conversion parts have been installed according to the

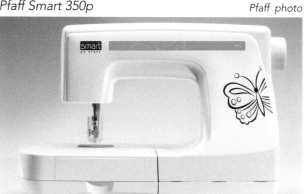

Pfaff Smart 350p   *Pfaff photo*

Sewing with Nancy Fab Felter

Nancy's Notions photo

directions, test for adequate clearance for the multiple needles by turning the hand wheel slowly so the needles go down into the hole in the needle plate. If there are no horrible sounds of metal on metal, you're good to go with the felting process.

Bernina

Some Bernina sewing machines can be adapted to needle felting by using the Decorative Needle Punch Attachment. Check with a dealer to see the current machines that can be modified.

The attachment requires the total removal of the bobbin mechanism and the installation of a special stitch plate to accommodate the barbed needle head. Up to five needles may be used for free-motion felting, and they can be removed/replaced individually.

Brother

Brother PQ series machines can be converted for felting by installing the Needle Felting Attachment kit. It contains five barbed needles, a special needle plate to accommodate the multiple needles and a clear acrylic presser foot/finger guard. In addition, the kit contains a dust box that replaces the machine's bobbin mechanism and collects the lint generated from the felting process, and a thread take-up cover. As a bonus, several colors of wool roving are included in the kit to get you started.

The presser foot height is adjustable for thick fibers, and if you're felting yarn, the presser foot has a built-in yarn guide for easy feeding.

If a needle breaks, a new head must be purchased for this machine, as needles cannot be replaced individually. The five needles must be used together for all felting.

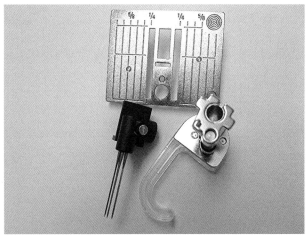

Bernina Decorative Needle Punch attachment.

Brother International photos

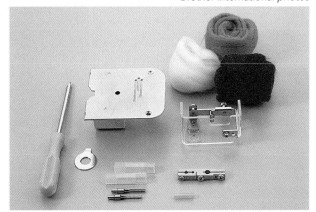

Brother Needle Felting attachment kit.

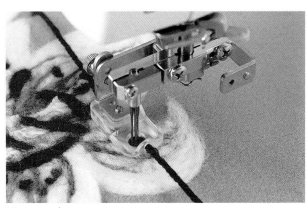

Yarn guide

Felting Flowers

The machine felting process is fast and easy, and these step-by-steps will show you how. All photos courtesy of Bernina of America, Inc.; artist: Faith Reynolds.

Create felted flowers like these by following the steps outlined below.

Add a different color for the flower base and stem.

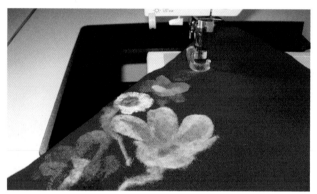

Continue adding flowers and punching in place.

Loop yarn or roving into a petal shape and secure it with punching.

When the front side is completed, punch from the back side to further lock the fibers.

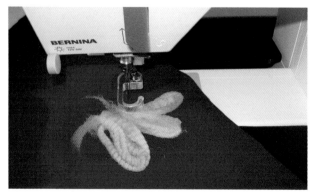

Continue shaping and punching petals.

Trim the excess fabric along the flower outlines.

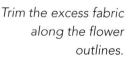

CHAPTER 7
Covering the Bases

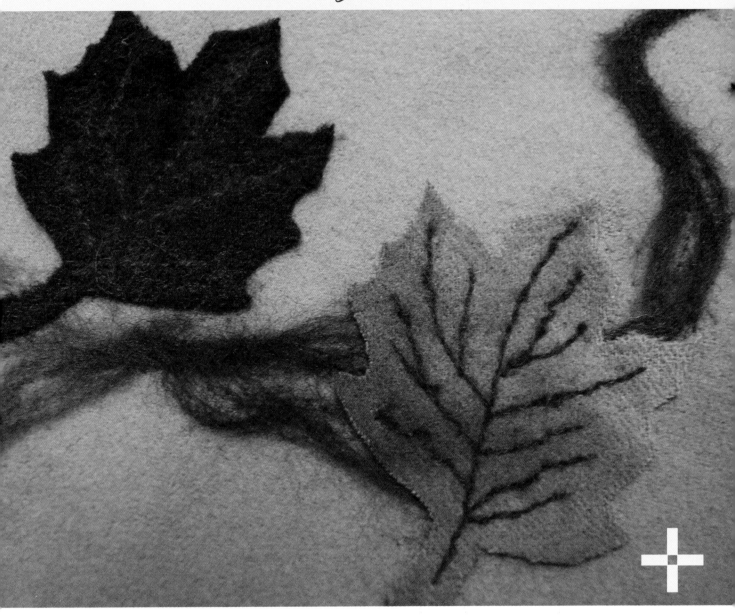

One of the fun things about needle felting is that the processes

can be combined with many other embellishing techniques.

From making appliqués to accenting machine embroidery,

there's great potential for multi-media creativity.

Appliqué

In addition to felting fabric in place onto a base, you can create freestanding appliqués with needle felting. These motifs can then be totally felted to a base or some portion of them left free, like cascading leaves along the edge of a table runner. In addition to joining them to a base, they can be used for dimensional work. For example, those same leaves can be sprinkled along a Thanksgiving table.

By making an appliqué, the repeated punching goes into a separate base and not the garment or project to which it is applied. Freestanding pieces then need to be felted only around the edges to hold them in place.

Why use this technique? If the project is made from a delicate fabric, needle felted appliqués minimizes the repeated punching needed to create them from damaging the fabric. It also allows you to create some dimension if you prefer that to flat motifs, as freestanding designs don't have to be felted flat to the base–they can be curled, folded, tucked or only partially attached.

Cactus Punch photo; design pack EP015

Machine embroider felt shapes and add needle felting accents.

Something on Nothing

To make a free-standing felted motif, use water-soluble stabilizer, felt or fabric as the base. Needle felt the design, then trim the base close to the edges of the felted motif. If water-soluble stabilizer is used, follow the manufacturer's instructions to get rid of any stabilizer that shows, and allow to dry thoroughly. If felt is the base, it doesn't ravel, so close trimming is all that's needed to finish the edges.

To attach all or part of a motif to the base, needle felt around the edges to hold it in place. Be thorough and felt enough to secure and blend the fibers.

For more information on this technique, see On the Rocks on page 112.

Embroidery

If you have an embroidery machine, entire designs or portions of them may be used with felting. It's important to ask the company about this use before you assume that they are fair game, as some designs are accompanied by licensing restrictions relating to their use. For example, it may not acceptable to alter the design in any way. Disney licensed motifs carry a number of restrictions, as do other character images, so ask before you needle felt Mickey Mouse onto your next sweatshirt to wear on your trip to the theme park.

Designer Marlis Bennett used needle felting to fill in an embroidered design.

Coloring Cues

Embroidered motifs can serve as an outline for fill-in felting, or they can be a portion of the felted design, such as the stitched stems and leaves for the felted flowers on the Eyeglass Elegance (see page 65).

Fabric Prints

Black & White

Remember the childhood admonitions about staying within the lines of a color book drawing? Wipe that from your thoughts if you didn't like the concept to begin with.

Black and white fabric prints provide the perfect canvas for needle felting. The patterning is already there and you can fill in the designs with fibers—all of them, or just a few sections, as your heart desires. Cover the lines, or stay within them—needle felting is so easy, you can cover the entire fabric if you want to.

Depending on the weight and weave of the base fabric, you may want to back it first with fusible interfacing for added stability to hold dense felting, and/or wait until you're done felting, then back it with interfacing to hold the fibers in place.

If you don't think of yourself as an artist, let someone else take on that role, and you accent their work with fibers.

Selecting a printed fabric as your felting base offers a ready-made color grouping. You can felt as much or as little of the print as you want to in similar colors, or go wild with color opposites, allowing no portions of the original color print to show through.

Felting portions of a print is a fun way to add dimensional hair, animal manes or ruffs, etc. for a bit of whimsy.

These stick figures were drawn with a bleach pen on denim to remove the dye and then the details were needle felted to add color and interest.

Dancing Needleworks photo

Designer Tricia Anderson used free-motion stitching with 12-wt. thread to accent Skeeters Bag.

Free-Motion Stitching

Whether you're working with wool or another not-so-feltable-on-its-own fiber, you can always help hold the fibers in place with some free-motion stitching over the surface.

To do free-motion stitching, simply lower the feed dogs on the sewing machine and move your creation around freely underneath the presser foot. Some machines have special feet for free-motion work that offer greater visibility than standard feet.

This is a great way to showcase some novelty threads in your work and to secure other fabric bits, yarns and trims that weren't felted into the base.

If you felt into water-soluble stabilizer, free-motion overstitching also helps to hold fibers in place after the dissolution process.

Inkjet Fabric Printing

In much the same way as you'd felt a ready-made fabric print, you can customize a family photo, clip-art or other design that you print yourself onto fabric. Simply follow the manufacturer's instructions for printing, then felt the parts you want to accent.

You can cover the entire fabric, or add fibers to only portions of it.

Clip-art and outline motifs can be used the same as an iron-on needlework transfer providing lines for you to fill in with a variety of felting techniques.

Note: For more information about inkjet fabric printing, see *Print Your Own Fabric* by Linda Turner Griepentrog and Missy Shepler, also published by Krause Publications.

Playing with Paper

Who said that needle felting only works on fabric? Using a single needle, either by hand or by machine, you can felt yarns or fibers onto paper to create tags, cards, stationery, etc.

The paper needs to be the fairly sturdy, hand-made variety with a high fiber content to support the repeated punching without perforating.

It's best to use twisted fibers or yarn to embellish papers, as they don't require the close needle stabs that loose fibers and untwisted roving does. Use a size 38 or larger needle, as the barbs are large enough to carry the fibers through the paper's surface. The more you puncture the paper, the more chance there is for permanent visible damage.

If the felted fibers appear loose, add a thin coating of glue on the underside or fusible interfacing to hold them in place and cover the back with a coordinating paper lining.

Fabric Painting

Combining fabric painting with needle felting may seem like a stretch, as you're not painting the fibers (though you could!). It's fun to create fiber shapes with felting and then stamp or paint coordinating motifs with paint.

Choose a paint that covers the fabric surface well for the best color reproduction, and embellish the stamped motifs with needle felting. Paint can be applied over felted fibers or used as a base for felted embellishments.

ScrapSmart Woodland Creatures image; skunk; The Vintage Workshop, Inkjet Printable Cotton Canvas

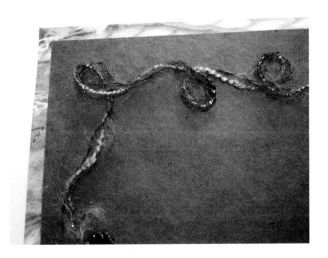

Stamp a motif and add felt accents. Jacquard Products Lumiere paint adds a touch of metallic to the look.

Beads sewn amongst the fibers accent the needle felting yarns.

Add-ins

Metallics

Metallic fibers make great accents when used in combination with other fibers. When used alone, metallic fibers do not felt. Many are smooth, flat fragile ribbons of metallic film with nothing to catch the fabric base's fibers. You can poke them into the base, but they may pop right back out at you!

The solution? Mix them with wool or other felt-able fibers that have "grab." You can twist the fibers together, or simply felt them together as you work through the design. The higher percentage of wool to metallics, the more secure the felted result will be.

Heavy metallic yarns or threads may be constructed with another fiber in the center, then wrapped with metallic. Be cautious in working with these yarns to avoid splitting or breaking the wrapping threads and exposing the center core, as the appearance can become ugly with the separation.

Beads

Beads can be incorporated into your felting projects in two ways: added after base felting is done and sewn onto the surface, or threaded onto yarn strands before or during the felting process. Adding beads while felting will allow for more needle breakage, as you may hit a bead while felting.

To actually incorporate beads into the felting, thread several onto a strand of yarn. The bead holes need to be large enough to slide along the strand length, pick beads up and slide them as you felt the yarn between.

Begin threading the beads on the yarn end farthest from the felting starting point, and slide one bead at a time toward the felted area. Use a single needle to felt beyond the bead, then slide the next one into place and repeat the process, anchoring one bead at a time.

If you prefer to showcase multiple beads, slide them forward each time before anchoring in place with the felted yarn.

This technique can also work with large-hole sequins or paillettes, flat Mylar disks with a single hole in them.

For step-by-steps on beading fringe, see Wrap it Up on page 70.

Buttons

Needle felting and novelty buttons are a natural combo. Felt a stem and a few leaves and add flower buttons, or felt a project and embellish the entire thing with button accents.

Scraps of needle felting are perfect to cover buttons as well—for more information on this technique, see Button, Button ... on page 106.

Glow-in-the-Dark Threads

This special thread can add interest to a felted piece that will be displayed or worn in low light or at a party using black light. The thread is specially treated to hold its luminescence for up to 15 hours, depending on the brand.

Like metallic threads, these novelty strands cannot be felted on their own, but they can be combined with other fibers to add a touch of glow-in-the-dark fun.

Colors of glow-in-the-dark threads vary from white, purple and peach to eerie lime, and one type is a glowable metallic for double shine. Look for these novelties with machine embroidery supplies.

Cover-Ups

For a more subtle look to needle felting, use it as a textural base and then cover it with a sheer fabric or netting for added interest. The covering fabric can be folded, pleated or tucked for dimension, or embellished with beads, sequins or other jewels for a bit of bling.

Using a fabric over felting will tone down the fiber colors, and depending on the color of the overlay, the color can appear quite different from the original.

Background Check

Needle felting can be used as a background for embroidery, either by hand or machine. Lightweight coverage works well for adding just a hint of color, but heavier coverage can be used to actually create the background fabric to accent the embroidery.

This is a great way to use some fibers that don't felt on their own (like metallics), as the overstitching holds them in place securely.

On the Edge

Cutting Cues

Depending on the fiber and weave of the needle felting base, you can use the actual felting as the edge embellishment, trimming the base just outside the felted area. On densely woven fabrics, there will be no raveling. On fabric bases that may be likely to ravel, use a seam sealant on the edges to prevent fraying.

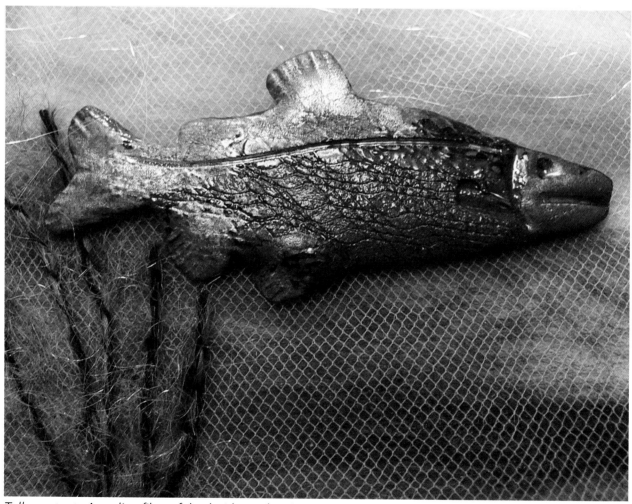

Tulle protects Angelina fibers felted with wool rovings.

Decorative Cutting

Many base fabrics used for felting are densely woven or knitted and do not require any edge finishes. Melton, coatings and felt can be left raw or finished, depending on the project. A fun edge treatment is to use a novelty rotary cutter blade to trim the project perimeter–the blades come with waves, scallops or pinking edges. We've used decoratively cut edges on several projects.

Fringe

A quick edge finish can be created using yarn and simple needle felting to anchor loops along a project edge. Yarn loops may be clipped if desired after the felting is completed.

Shape loops freehand making the fringe as dense or sparse as you prefer, depending on the project.

If you want to dress up the fringe, thread beads onto the yarn strands. For step-by-step directions, see Wrap it Up on page 70.

Olfa Rotary Cutter & Decorative Blades

Picot Edges

Similar to fringe felting, a picot edge is formed by felting small yarn loops to the fabric edge at regular intervals. Mark dots with chalk for consistent spacing. Like fringe, be sure to felt the yarn in place from both sides for durability. This technique requires the use of a single hand needle.

CHAPTER 8
Fabulously Frugal Felting

In addition to using needle felting for decorative purposes,

it can also be used for utilitarian purposes like mending. Fabrics can be recycled

to use as felting bases and needle felted items can be wet felted to give them

a different look. Read on for more details on these ideas...

Mending

Got a moth hole in a favorite wool sweater or pair of jeans and darning just doesn't seem like a very exciting idea? Use your needle felting skills to cover the hole decoratively and no one will be the wiser.

But first, note the hole location to be sure it's appropriate for embellishing. Avoid calling attention to bust points and derriere cheeks with needle felted motifs. Other locations are workable, however.

Depending on the size of the hole, you may need to mend the hole before you begin felting or use some kind of base fabric or stabilizer behind it to add stability. A small piece of stabilizer placed behind the hole can serve as an anchor point for initial felting, with the fibers worked out in the design to include the actual garment fabric. Temporary spray adhesive can hold the patch in place, or simply hand-baste. Excess stabilizer is trimmed around the motif when the felting is complete.

Felted Bases

Though the primary focus of this book is on dry felting techniques, you may want to use your washing machine to create a dense, firm base for the needle felting process.

Almost any fabric that is at least 70% wool will felt in a washer—varying degrees depending on the exact fiber content. Start with yardage or garments; wool sweaters are ideal for the wet-felting process, as the knit structure compacts nicely.

Be sure the label on your fabric or garment doesn't say it's washable wool, or "ready for the needle" as these indicate the fabric has been specially treated in the manufacturing process and they will not felt under normal washing conditions.

How much will something shrink and felt? There's no way to know without making a sample. If it's important to know an exact amount of shrinkage, cut

Designer Terry Weiss felted a scene to hide moth holes on this wool vest.

Thrifty designer Dorothy Akiyama used chunky yarns to hide damage to a thrift store sweater neckline.

a 12" square of the fabric and wash it as described below, then remeasure it to determine the shrink percentage.

Machines in Motion

Hot water, dish soap and agitation are the magic ingredients that make wool fibers shrink and felt together. It's a permanent process and you may have done it unintentionally to a wool sweater that erroneously made its way to the laundry basket.

The easiest method for felting wool fabric is to use a washing machine. Wash the fabric or sweater in hot water and agitate it for 10 minutes. Check for the amount of shrinkage, and if more felting is needed, continue the agitation process, checking frequently to avoid overfelting.

When you're happy with the amount of shrinkage, put the base fabric into a hot dryer or lay flat to dry for finished items.

It's a simple process and always fun to see what happens to different types of fabric or sweatering, as the results are not predictable. Items with the highest wool content will compact the most.

What is sweatering?

Sweatering is fabric harvested from old sweaters, or it can also refer to sweater yardage sold on a bolt.

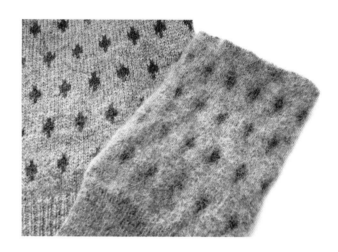

Washed wools look entirely different from their original pieces. Notice the disappearance of a visible weave or knit patterns once the fibers are compacted.

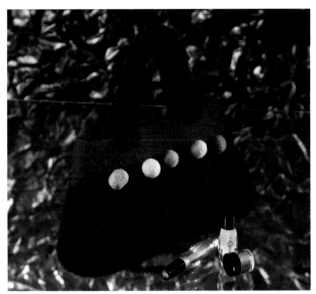

Avid knitter Laura Rintala created this two-tone bag and machine felted it in the washer. Wet-felted beads were added as accents after the shrinking process. For more information on making felted beads, see Round & Round on page 116.

Knit Wits

If you're a knitter, you can felt your creations using the same technique outlined above. It's important to test-felt a swatch before beginning your project so that you know how oversized to knit for good results. A 12"-square swatch in the same gauge as your work is perfect for the testing process.

Needle felting can be done on hand knits before they are felted, or after, depending on the look you prefer.

To try wet felting a sweater project embellished with needle felting, see the Knit Wits knitting needle case on page 83.

Thrift Store Chic

Thrift stores can be a mecca for felters–just walk down the sweater and garment aisles (men's, women's and children's) and feel for wool. Double-check the labels as many acrylics can be easily mistaken for wools. Look for 100% wool for the best felting characteristics, but some blends may also work. Remember, the higher the wool content, the more the piece will felt.

If your thrift store has poundage areas (sometimes at double/triple discounts), this is a great place to find feltable items. Yardage sections can often yield uncut wool fabrics, ready for felting.

Bigger is Better

The men's and plus-size departments
are great places to look for wool sweaters
and garments you plan to felt, as
you'll get more yardage.

Don't forget about the home décor areas
as well — you could find a great wool
blanket — hopefully king-size!

Fiber-lover Alyce Thomson used a felted sweater as the base for her coiled motif bag. Note how the original sweater ribbing is used as the purse flap.

Projects

Eyeglass Elegance

Protecting your glasses is important and this flowery case is the perfect way to showcase your felting skills and safeguard your lenses at the same time. Dimensional beaded flowers accent the embroidered leaves.

Finished size: 6½" x 4"

MATERIALS

Note: This project is best done with hand felting.

9" x 12" melton cloth or felt

⅜ yd. silk doupioni, 45" wide

Sewing, embroidery* and bobbin thread

Loosely twisted variegated yarn

Tear-away stabilizer*

Seed beads

Felting needle

Foam or brush base

Beading needle

Straight pins

Air-disappearing marker

Temporary spray adhesive*

Embroidery machine

Leaf/stem machine embroidery designs*

Note: If you don't have an embroidery machine, use hand embroidery to create similar leaves and stems.

*Used in this project: Sulky of America, 40-wt. rayon embroidery thread, Tear-Easy Stabilizer and KK2000 Spray Adhesive; Husqvarna Viking, embroidery disk 36 (Summer Flowers), design 27

Cutting

Depending on the size of your glasses, adjust the pattern accordingly. Using the pattern shown 66, cut one case from melton cloth and one from the silk doupioni.

Cut the remaining silk into 2¼" bias strips for binding, piecing if needed to make 30".

Embroidery

1 Using embroidery software or on-screen editing, combine the design motif sections and adjust the size to fit your case. Mark the design center point on the case front.

2 Hoop the tear-away stabilizer and spray the underside of the wool case with temporary adhesive. Adhere the case to the hooped stabilizer, matching the design center point to the hoop placement markings.

3 Embroider the leaf portion of the design only, ignoring the flowers.

4 Tear away the stabilizer and trim all the jump threads.

Fold Line

Front

1 Square = 1 inch

Felting

1 Place the case over the foam/brush base and position six pins in a circle ½" larger than the desired size of the flower. Pin the yarn at the flower center to anchor it. Work with one flower at a time for best results.

2 Loosely wrap the yarn around the pins for consistent petal sizing. The yarn will pull in slightly as it's felted, so don't wrap it too tightly around the pins.

3 Felt the flower center only, leaving the petals as dimensional loops. Remove the guide pins once the center is felted.

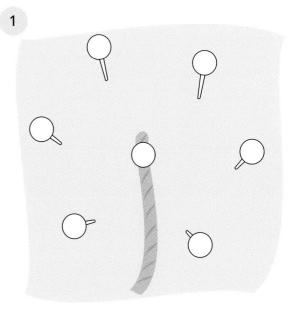

Position guide pins for flower placement.

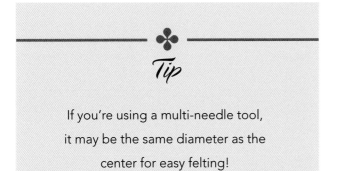

♣

Tip

If you're using a multi-needle tool, it may be the same diameter as the center for easy felting!

4 Using a contrasting portion of the yarn, place a small bit of it in the flower center and felt into place.

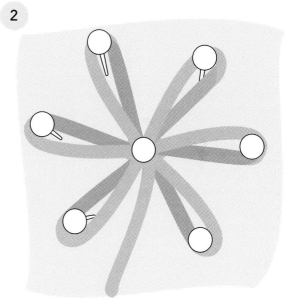

Wrap yarn loosely around the pins.

Construction

1 Sew several seed beads at the flower centers.

2 Spray the underside of the wool case with temporary adhesive and adhere to the doupioni, matching the cut edges. Baste in place 1/8" from the edges.

3 Bind the edges of the case, mitering the corners and easing the bias around the curved portion to avoid puckers.

4 Fold the case in half aligning the lower and side edges. Hand stitch the case side and lower edges together between the binding layers, ending 4" from the lower corner.

Hand stitch the layers together between the binding.

Wrap it Up

Wrap it Up

This simple double-sided scarf makes a great first project and the yarn on both sides extends into beaded fringe. A patterned fabric weave can provide ready-made yarn placement lines or draw your own on solid yardage.

Finished size: 10" x 60", excluding fringe

MATERIALS

⅓ yd. lightweight wool, 60" wide

Loosely twisted, or untwistable yarn*

Iridescent beads, 3mm diameter

Needle threader*

Air-disappearing marker (optional)

Felting needle, multi-needle tool or felting machine

Foam or brush base (for hand felting)

*Used in this project: Lion Brand Yarns, Fettuccini, Starburst; Klaer International, Ultra-Fine threader

Cutting

Tear the wool into a 10"-wide strip across the fabric width and cut off the selvages.

Felting

1 If the wool has a patterned weave, use that as a yarn placement guide. If not, use a removable marker to mark placement lines evenly spaced starting 1½" from each scarf torn edge.

2 If the yarn has a wrapping thread or stitching holding it together, remove that so it can fluff.

3 Place the scarf fabric over a foam or brush base if felting by hand.

Quick Tip

If felting by machine, lightly pin the yarns in place as you position them, but remove the pins before you felt that area.

4 Allow 4" of yarn for fringe at one end of the scarf and begin felting the yarn along the placement lines. Use the lines/weave only as a guide—it's okay to meander slightly for interest. Felt the yarn securely and leave 4" of yarn free at the opposite end for fringe.

5 Repeat the felting process for all the lines.

6 Turn the scarf over and position additional yarn strands over the previously felted yarn, using it as a placement guide. Felt the second-side yarns in place as noted above, leaving the ends free for fringe.

Beading

1 Use a needle threader to thread the beads onto the individual yarn fringe strands and push them along to space evenly.

2 Trim the fringe ends evenly, if desired.

Yarn Note

The yarn used in this project is comprised of two strands of variegated fiber held together with a serger stitch. Before beginning the project, we removed the stitching to separate the yarns and then untwisted them to expose more fiber surface. Remember to take a close look at yarns to see what they might become, not just how they look when you purchase them!

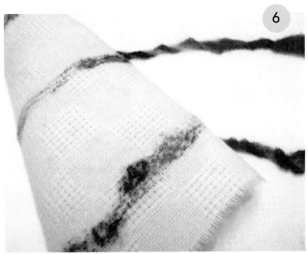

Use the previously felted lines as a placement guide for side 2.

Place the bead onto the needle threader wire.

Slide the tip of the fringe yarn end through the tip of the threader wire (a few fibers is all you need).

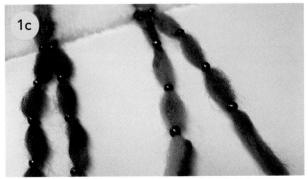

Gently pull the bead onto the yarn and slide it into place.

On the Flip Side

Needle felting creates textural interest on both sides of the base fabric and this clever bag actually showcases the underside of the work. Read more about the clever "stained glass" patterning technique.

Finished size: 11" x 11" x 2", excluding handles

MATERIALS

½ yd. black wool coating, 60" wide

Note: Black wool is key to having the technique look like stained glass.

½ yd. print lining, 45" wide

½ yd. fusible heavy craft interfacing, 30" wide*

Note: If interfacing is narrower, more will be needed.

Multiple bright colors wool roving

Paper-back fusible web*

Black sewing thread

Felting needle, multi-needle tool and/or felting machine

Foam or brush base (for hand felting)

Note: This project requires a single hand felting needle to create sharp design edges.

Blue painter's tape, ½" wide
(*Note:* Do not substitute masking tape.)

U-shape purse handles, 4" inside span

*Used in this project: The Warm Company, Steam-A-Seam2 paper-backed fusible web; RNK Distributing, Floriani Stitch N Shape heavy craft interfacing

Cutting

From the black wool, cut a rectangle at least 17" x 28" for the base. The actual bag will be cut once the felting is completed. For the handle attachments, cut a 1½" x 12" strip of fabric.

From the lining fabric, cut one bag using the pattern shown on page 74.

Felting

1 On one end of the fabric wrong side, use the painter's tape to mask off a grid that will be the "leading" between the color panels and place the tape around the perimeter design edges in the shape shown on the bag front. Position the design at least 2" from the base fabric end. Be sure the tape is firmly adhered to the wool so you can felt against it for crisp edge lines.

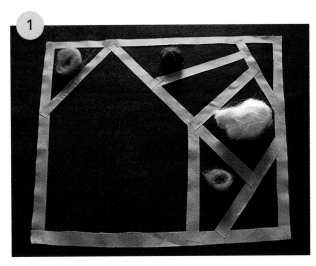

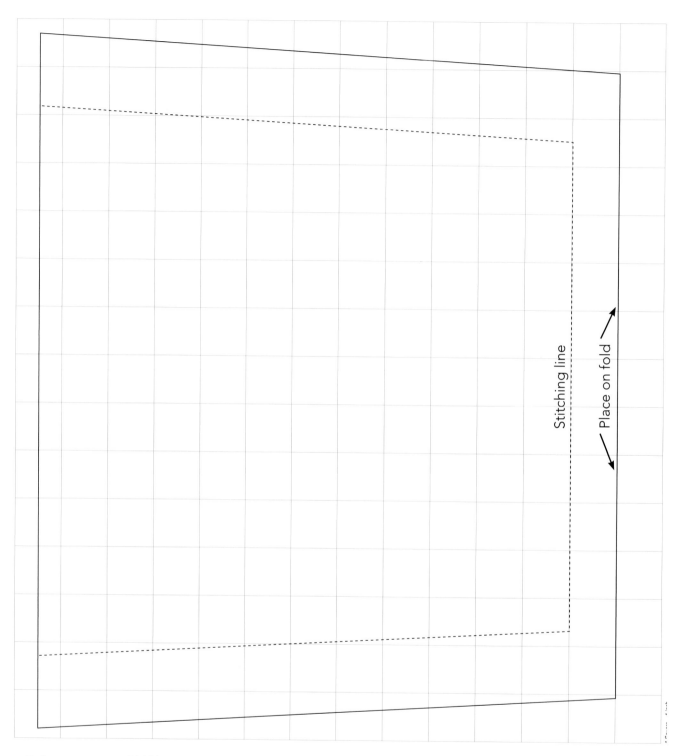

Stitching line

Place on fold

Enlarge pattern 200%

2 Select wool roving colors and separate fibers into wisps for felting. If desired, photocopy the pattern and use colored pencils or markers to note color segment placement on the bag front.

3 Begin the felting process on the fabric wrong side using a single hand needle to shape the roving and create sharp corners. A felting tool or machine may be used to fill in the panes once the roving is secure and shaped.

4 When the initial felting is complete, turn the fabric over and felt again to further entangle the fibers. The exposed felting is actually the wrong side as the felting process was done, offering a more muted look to the design area. Either side may be used as the outside, depending on the look you like.

5 Carefully remove the painter's tape, being careful not to pull out any felted fibers.

Construction

All seam allowances are ½", unless otherwise noted.

1 Lay the bag pattern on the felted wool and trim to the pattern size, centering the felted panel on the bag front portion of the pattern.

2 Back the entire bag panel with stiff craft interfacing and press in place firmly.

3 To create the bag corners, stitch along the dashed lines and bend the interfacing to crease.

4 Right sides together, sew the bag side seams and press the seam allowances open. If you have a sleeve board, use it to access the seam area; if not, roll up a magazine, cover it with a towel and slip it inside the bag under the seams. Press firmly with the iron and use a steam setting to set the seams open.

5 To box the bag lower corners, fold the bag right sides together, centering the side seam across the bag bottom; draw a 2"-wide line and stitch through all layers.

3   *Interfacing*

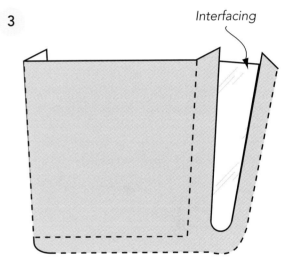

Stitch to create crease lines.

5

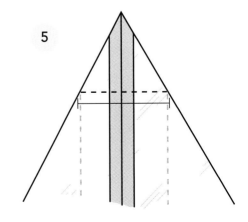

Box the lower bag corners.

6 Right sides together, construct the lining following the same instructions as the bag, except leave a 7" opening in one side seam for turning and don't stitch the corner lines. Box the lining corners as you did for the outer bag.

6

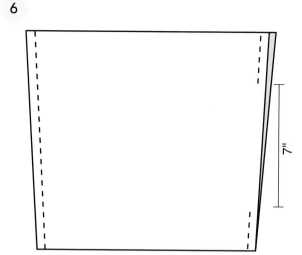

Leave opening for turning.

7 To make the handle loops, place a strip of paper-back fusible web on the underside of the fabric rectangle and trim to size. Lightly fuse following the manufacturer's instructions. Peel the paper backing off the web strip and fold the fabric into thirds; fuse again creating a ½"-wide strip. *Note:* Check the width of your handle opening and adjust the strip width if needed prior to the final fusing. Cut the strip into four 2½" lengths.

8

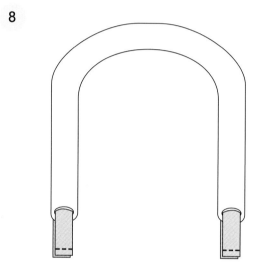

8 Place the loops through the bag handles with the cut edges inside. Using a zipper foot, stitch the raw edges together.

Attach fabric loops to the handles.

9 With the cut edges together, baste the handles to the bag front and back upper edges 4" apart, and centered within the design area right side.

9

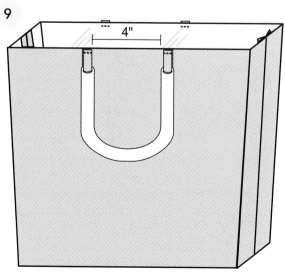

Baste the handles to the bag front and back centers.

10 Right sides together, slip the lining into the bag and pin the upper edges, matching the side seams. Stitch the lining to the bag and carefully pull the bag right side out through the opening, being careful of the handles.

11 Tuck the lining into the bag and press the upper edge firmly, rolling under the lining seam slightly. Work around the handles as you press and avoid touching them with the iron, as the plastic may melt. Topstitch the upper purse edge, rolling the lining slightly to the inside of the bag as you stitch. Hand sew the lining opening closed or use fusible web for a faster closing.

Quick Tip

This stained glass technique would make a lovely pincushion too! See Pins 'n' Needles on page 103 for directions.

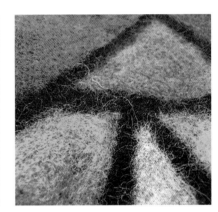

Inside Scoop

Help a bag keep its shape by adding some inner structure. There are several brands of stiff craft interfacings available and some are fusible. Fusible varieties include single- and double-sided versions, depending on the project needs. The featured bag uses a single-sided fusible to help stiffen the felted wool. Double-sided fusible stiffeners are used for things like place mats and fabric bowls where they are sandwiched between two fabrics. Follow the manufacturer's instructions for fusing and use a non-stick press cloth to prevent adhesive from damaging your iron's soleplate.

Double Duty

Always test-felt a sample before you begin a project to see how the fabric and fibers work together, and if you like the finished look. At that time, check which side you like best, and remember, both sides of felting look different and there is no right or wrong—it's your choice.

Autumn Leaves

❖

*Add a touch of fall to a custom-sewn (or ready-made) vest
using wool leaf appliqués cascading down the one side.
Note the detailed leaf veins created with faux-stitch felting.*

Finished size: custom

MATERIALS

Assorted hand-dyed harvest-tone wool scraps for 8 leaves

Finished wool vest*

Large button

Large snap

Slubby yarn, variegated fall colors*

Assorted fall colors of needle punch yarn

Single felting needle and multi-needle tool or felting machine

Foam or brush base (for hand needle felting)

Lightweight fusible interfacing

*Used in this project: Nashua Yarn, Painted Forest, Red Berries; Stitchery Safe, My Favorite Vest pattern

Cutting

Cut and construct the wool vest according to the pattern instructions.

(*Note:* A ready-made vest can be substituted, but avoid design lines and seaming to interrupt the felting area.)

Cut 8 leaves from assorted fall colors of wools using the pattern below.

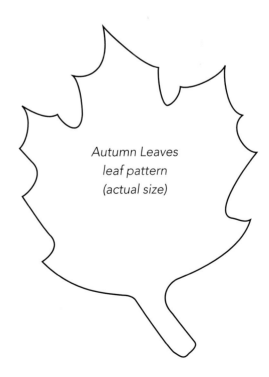

*Autumn Leaves
leaf pattern
(actual size)*

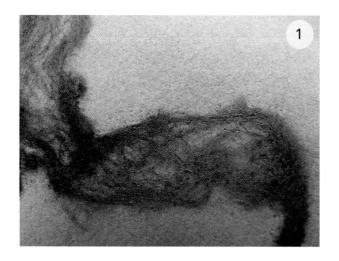

Felting

1 Gently pull apart the slubby yarn and untwist it to form gauzy fibers. Position the open yarn meandering along the vest front, up and over the shoulder area and about 6" down the back. Feather the yarn at both ends to finish.

Note: The design details will depend on the vest style and size; use the photograph as a guide and adapt the techniques to your vest.

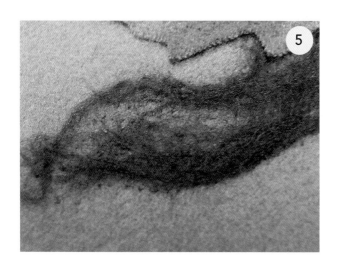

2 Using a felting tool or felting machine, lightly "baste" the yarns in place.

3 Pin the leaves in place as desired, varying the colors for interest.

4 Using a single needle, "baste" the leaves in place. Try on the vest and adjust the placement of yarn and/or leaves if desired.

5 Thoroughly felt the yarn and leaves in place from both sides using a multi-needle tool or a felting machine. The leaf edges may be left unfelted for dimension, if desired.

6 To create the leaf vein detailing, use needle punch yarn. Position the yarn down the leaf center and use a single felting needle to push it into the fabric. Move the needle forward ½" and insert the needle's barbed tip into the yarn to grab it. Gently pull the yarn back ¼" toward the first stitch. Push the yarn through the appliqué and into the base fabric forming a visible "stitch." The yarn should be pushed completely through both fabric layers and a small loop should be visible on the vest underside. Repeat the process to detail the leaf veins.

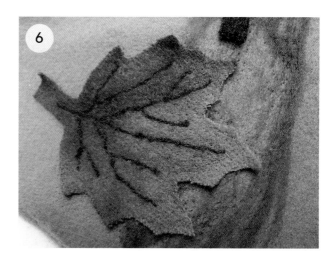

7 When all the detail stitching is complete, turn the vest over and use a multi-needle tool or a felting machine to felt from the backside. Turn over again and repeat the felting process from the right side.

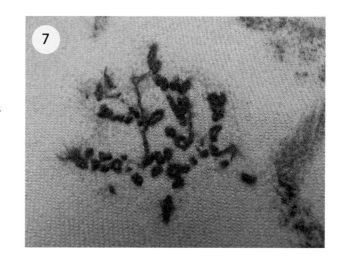

8 Back the vest appliqué areas with fusible interfacing to secure them and the detail stitching in place.

9 Sew the decorative button on the vest overlap and stitch a snap underneath it for closing.

Knit Wits

Having a great case to store your knitting needles couldn't be more fun that creating your own from a wool sweater and some fabulous yarns. This project, which holds 8 pair of 14"-long needles, utilizes wet felting combined with needle felting for added fun.

Finished size: 12" x 15", closed

MATERIALS

Off-white lightweight rib-knit wool sweater, prefelted

Note: Any wool sweater of your choice can be used.

Several earthtone wool or wool/silk rovings

Note: Rovings with bits of raw silk add texture and contrast color flecks.

⅞ yd. cotton print for lining and binding, 45"-wide

3-ply tapestry wool*

1-ply needle punch yarn

Assorted seed, twisted bugle and facet beads

Felting needle, multi-needle tool or felting machine

Foam or brush base (for hand felting)

Sewing and beading thread

Hand beading needle

Air-disappearing marker

Temporary spray adhesive*

Heavy plastic to cover work surface

Rolling pin

Bubblewrap

Absorbent towels

Liquid dish soap (not detergent)

*Used in this project: DMC Tapestry Wool; Sulky of America, KK2000 spray adhesive

Cutting

From the felted sweater, cut a 14" x 20" rectangle. *Note:* It's important that the sweater has already been felted before beginning this project, or it will shrink more with the wet felting of the design. If it isn't pre-felted, cut a larger rectangle to allow for additional shrinkage.

From the cotton fabric, cut the following rectangles: 12" x 18" for the lining, 12" x 28" for the pocket; and enough 2¼" wide bias to make 3¼ yards, piecing as needed.

Dry Felting

1 Use the air-disappearing marker to sketch a marsh design on the sweater knit right side.

2 Begin the design by positioning the larger leaves, twisting the rovings to create the desired effect and create some shading. Add details and smaller leaves/branches/stems with the smaller yarns, untwisting as needed. Feather the yarn ends at the tip of the leaves. As you build the scene, it may be necessary to lift a portion of one leaf to slide another underneath. Felt the entire marsh into place.

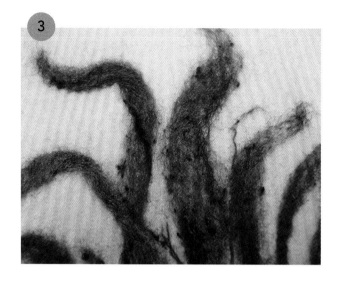

3 Create the base using green and brown rovings pulled thinly across the sweater base, feathering out the ends to fade at the edges. Felt in place.

4 Fashion a rock by winding a small loose ball of brown roving and then felting it in place. Add lighter, thinner yarns for detailing. Felt in place.

Wet Felting

1 Working outside or in a laundry room, cover the work surface with heavy plastic and position the felted scene on it. Mix 1 quart of warm water with 1 teaspoon of liquid soap.

2 Pour the soapy water over the felted scene and cover with a layer of thin Bubblewrap. Place the covered fabric around a rolling pin and roll back and forth for several minutes to work the soapy water into the sweatering.

3 When the roving fibers are thoroughly embedded in the fabric surface, rinse the piece in clear, cool water to remove the soap. Do not wring. Place the wet fabric onto a towel and press out the excess water using another towel on top of it. Shape and allow to dry.

4 Steam-press the sweatering to block it into shape and allow to dry.

Construction

1 Cut the felted piece into a 12" x 18" rectangle, centering the design across the width.

2 Sew on the assorted beads as accents.

3 To make the needle pocket, fold the rectangle wrong sides together and press, forming a 14" x 12" double pocket. Mark lines for the pockets every 1½" across the pocket width. Position the pocket on the lining, matching raw edges. Stitch on the lines, backstitching at the upper pocket edge.

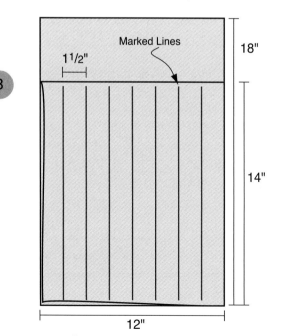

Create the pocket and attach to lining.

4 Spray the wrong side of the felted sweater piece with temporary adhesive and lightly press the pocketed lining in place, matching the cut edges; baste ⅛" from the edge.

5 To make the ties, cut two 24"-long pieces of bias out of cotton fabric. Fold both edges to the center; press and stitch the open edges together. Fold the remaining binding in half and press a crease.

6 With raw edges of the binding against the lining side of the case, bind the edges of the tote, mitering the corners as you reach them. Turn the bias binding to the sweater side and topstitch or hand sew in place.

7 Fold the ties in half and sew to the sweater side of the case, 4½" from the upper edge and 2½" from the lower edge.

8 Place the knitting needles in the pockets, fold the flap down to secure them in place, roll, tie and go!

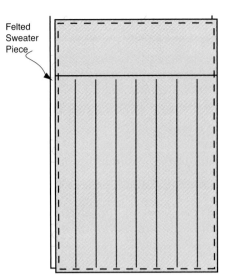

Match the lining/pocket to the outer case.

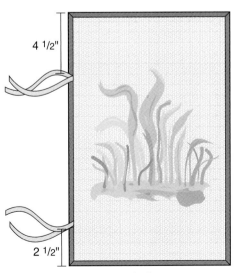

Bind the case edges, mitering corners.

Felted Sweater Piece

4

5

7

4 1/2"

2 1/2"

Attach the ties.

✛

Bead-dazzle it!

Adding beads to felting is easy and they add lots of glitz and depth to an otherwise flat design. Choose beads that are iridescent, faceted or twisted for maximum bling.

Bag It!

Whether you use it for make-up or a quick trip out, this mini-bag fills the bill.
The needle felted bead picks up the design colors and makes a handy zipper pull.

Finished size: 6" x 8"

MATERIALS

Prefelted sweater

Synthetic coil zipper, 16" long

¼ yd. lining fabric

Assorted colors needle punch and tapestry yarns

Small piece of roving

Chalk marker

¼ yd. double-face satin ribbon, ¼" wide

Soda straw

Fabric/craft glue*

Felting needle, multi-needle tool or felting machine

Foam/brush base (for hand felting)

Needle threader*

Hand sewing needle and thread

*Used in this project: Beacon Adhesives, Fabri-Tac Glue; Klaer International, Needlework Threader

Cutting

From the sweatering, cut one piece 7" x 17" with the ribbed edge along the length of the rectangle.

From the lining fabric, cut the same size rectangle.

Felting

1 Chalk-mark the design onto one half of the sweater rectangle, positioning it as desired.

1 Square = 1 inch

Position the design as desired on one-half of the bag length.

3

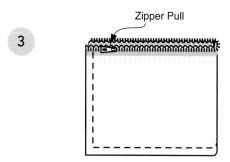

Zipper Pull

Join the side and lower bag seams.

4

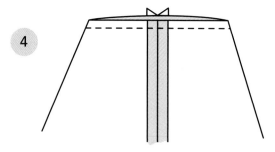

Box the bag corners.

2 Felt the design area, filling in the circle and the leaves with smaller yarns and outlining with contrast colors. Felt on both sides to secure. If the sweatering is not tightly felted, press fusible interfacing behind the motif to secure it.

Construction

1 Separate the zipper and remove the pull. Using one side of the zipper tape only, stitch it in place under the ribbed sweatering edge. It's very easy for this edge to stretch, so continually ease the sweater to fit the zipper length to avoid distortion.

2 Work the zipper pull back onto the zipper tapes and slide up and down to check for alignment. Leave the zipper partially open.

3 Right sides together, fold the sweater rectangle in half matching the short edges and stitch a ½" seam. Continue stitching across the lower edge, again easing the sweatering to avoid stretching.

4 Box the lower bag corners by centering the lower seam across the end seam; repeat the boxing for the opposite end judging the half-way point visually since there is no side seam.

5 Construct the lining like the bag, omitting the zipper. Press under ½" along the bag upper edge.

6 Wrong sides together, slip the lining into the bag and hand sew along the zipper tape.

Bead

1 Roll a small bit of roving around the straw and use a single needle to felt it to itself—avoid puncturing the straw if possible. Roll the bead that's forming around the straw to avoid creating something flat. Punch into a brush or foam base as you work, not the straw!

2 Continue adding roving and felting, mixing colors as desired. Shape the bead as you felt and add roving until the bead reaches the size needed.

3 When you're satisfied with the bead's shape and size, leave the bead on the straw and wet it, adding a small drop of soap.

4 Roll the wet bead onto a towel several times to round it, rinse and let dry with the straw in it.

5 Remove the bead from the straw when it's completely dry and thread it onto the ribbon using a needle threader; knot below the bead. Apply a small drop of glue inside the bead to permanently position it, using a straight pin to get the glue inside.

Ring in the Season

*The look of traditional crewelwork can be duplicated with needle felting
to make this versatile bell hanger. Whether you're showcasing an heirloom bell
or decorating a niche, it's a beautiful accent.*

Finished size: 5" x 13"

MATERIALS

¼ yd. white wool flannel, 54" wide

¼ yd. muslin, 45" wide

Assorted multi-color and needle punch yarns

5" x 13" double-sided fusible stiff craft interfacing*

Crewelwork iron-on transfer pattern*

Bell pull hardware set, 5"

1½" bell

Small jump ring

Paper-back fusible web tape, ½"-wide*

Felting needle and multi-needle tool

Note: This project is best felted by hand.

Foam/brush base

Non-stick press cloth

Needle-nose pliers

*Used in this project: RNK Distributing, Floriani Stitch N Shape heavy craft interfacing; Warm Company, Steam-A-Seam2 paper-back fusible web tape; Colonial Patterns, Aunt Martha's Iron-on Transfer, #3937 Blue Onion Motif

Preparation & Cutting

1 From the white wool, cut a 7" x 14" rectangle. From the muslin, cut a 5" x 13" rectangle.

2 Following the manufacturer's instructions, iron the transfer to the wool right side, centering the design along the rectangle length.

Felting

1 Using the yarn colors of your choice, fill in the defined spaces with yarns adding shading as desired.

2 Use contrasting yarns for outlining the shapes and needle punch yarns to felt the stems.

3 After felting the right side of the design, turn the piece over and felt from the underside to secure the yarns.

Construction

1 Center the felted piece over the interfacing rectangle, turning the raw wool edges to the back side. Cover the pressing surface with a towel to avoid flattening the felted motif as you fuse. Using the non-stick press cloth, fuse the wool to the interfacing being sure the design area is free of wrinkles.

2 Slide the ends of the wool through the bell pull hardware, fold under and use paper-back fusible web to hold them in place.

3 Fold under the edges of the muslin backing so the piece is just slightly smaller than the mounted crewel work. Apply paper-back fusible web to the hems, then fuse in place on the back of the hanging.

4 Using the jump ring, attach the bell to the bottom of the hanger loop.

Coloring Inside the Lines

*Tapestry fabric makes the perfect "canvas" for needle felting—
the pattern's already there and waiting for lovely yarns to fill it.
Needle felt all or part of the fabric pattern for this elegant bag.*

Finished size: 10" x 5" x 1½"

MATERIALS

½ yd. lightweight tapestry fabric, 54" wide

⅓ yd. lining fabric, 45" wide

Variegated yarn

Double-sided fusible stiff craft interfacing*

Magnetic purse closure, ⅝" diameter

Decorator tassel, 3"

Felting needle, multi-needle tool or felting machine

Foam/brush base (for hand felting)

Non-stick press cloth

Fabric/craft glue

* Used in this project: RNK Distributing, Floriani Stitch N Shape heavy craft interfacing; Crafter's Pick, The Ultimate! Glue

Tip

If your tapestry fabric is heavy,

select a larger size needle.

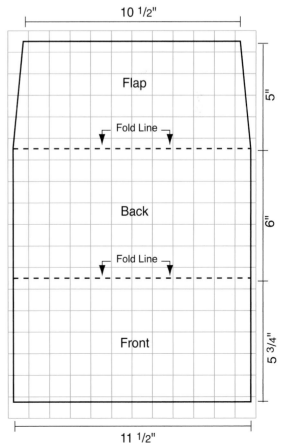

10 ½"

Flap

5"

Fold Line

Back

6"

Fold Line

Front

5 ¾"

11 ½"

1 Square = 1 inch

Cutting

1 From the tapestry fabric, lining and stiff craft interfacing, cut one bag using the pattern on page 93. If your tapestry has a definite patterning or decorative band, center that across the bag width.

2 Beginning 5" from the upper bag front, taper and trim the flap edges of the craft interfacing to 9" wide.

Felting

1 Using the tapestry pattern lines as a guide for patterning, felt within all or part of the motifs, allowing the tapestry print outlines to show as an edge. Use the variegation in the yarn to shade the design areas. *Note:* The featured bag shows a felted flap area only.

2 Turn the bag over and felt from the underside to anchor the yarns.

Construction

1 Using the non-stick press cloth, fuse the felted tapestry fabric to the stiff craft interfacing, allowing the excess fabric to overhang the flap edges on either side.

2 Press under ½" along the bag body upper edge. Fold the bag right sides together along the lower foldline and sew the side seams using ½" seams. Press open firmly, using a press cloth if needed to avoid melting the tapestry fabric.

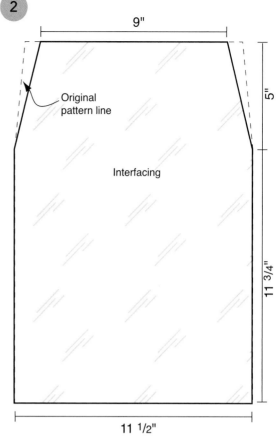

Shape the craft interfacing.

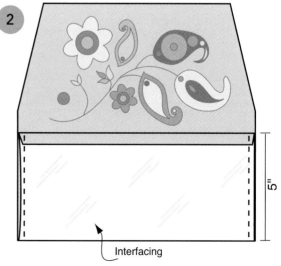

Sew the bag side seams.

3 To square the lower bag corners, fold the side seams to meet the bag bottom center. Draw a line 1½" long and stitch. Trim the excess fabric to reduce bulk.

4 Fold the excess tapestry flap fabric to the wrong side and fuse in place using the non-stick press cloth.

5 Construct the bag lining following the directions above for the bag but using a ⅝" seam allowance, pressing under ½" along the flap side and upper edges.

6 Following the manufacturer's instructions, apply the magnetic snap fasteners to the bag front and lining flap as shown. Slip the lining into the bag and hand sew in place. Press to fuse the lining to the fusible interfacing.

7 Glue the tassel in place on the bag front center lower edge. Snap and go!

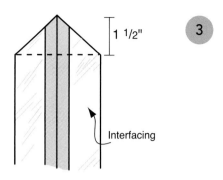

Box the bag corners.

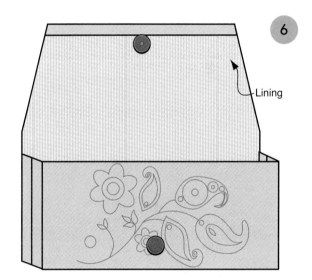

Apply the fasteners on opposite purse sections.

Flower Power

Make a coordinating outfit by creating flowers on a jacket that mimic the skirt fabric print. Remember that the actual fabric design is copyrighted, so you cannot copy the motifs exactly—use them only for inspiration.

Finished size: custom

MATERIALS

Finished wool jacket (or sweater) and skirt, readymade or custom made

Assorted rovings to mimic skirt print colors

Chalk marker

Felting needle, multi-needle tool or felting machine

Foam/brush base (for hand felting)

Felting

1 Draw a flower (or other motif) using the coordinating skirt fabric as inspiration. Simplify the lines if needed to make the felting process easier.

2 Chalk-mark the flower pattern onto the jacket front and back. Try on the jacket to double-check the placement and adjust if needed.

3 Using the skirt fabric as a guide, echo the shape and coloring as you felt the flowers and leaves onto the jacket. Shade the flower as desired for a more realistic look, or use less shading for a more graphic look, depending on your preference.

4 When the felting is completed on the right side, turn the jacket over and felt from the underside to secure the fibers. On loosely woven or knitted garments, fuse a small piece of interfacing over the underside side of the motifs to further secure the fibers.

5 If desired, add beads to accent the flowers.

Sheep Thrills

✕

*Curl up under this cozy throw while reading or watching TV.
It's lined for extra warmth and the cute sheep will make you smile—
and they're a good way to try out some fun felting techniques.*

Finished size: 45" x 60"

MATERIALS

1⅜ yd. red wool flannel, 60" wide

1⅜ yd. black curly fleece, 60" wide

¾ yd. black and white silk check, 60" wide

Assorted roving and yarns

Lamb machine embroidery design*

Tear-away stabilizer*

Embroidery, bobbin and sewing threads*

Temporary spray adhesive*

Felting needle, multi-needle tool or felting machine

Foam/brush base (for hand felting)

Chalk marker

Hand sewing needle

Note: An embroidery machine was used for this project; if you don't have one, see directions in Stitch it Up for more information.

*Used in this project: "Embroidery Machine Essentials, Quilting Techniques", 5" x 7" Lamb embroidery design; Sulky of America, KK2000 Spray Adhesive, 30-wt. rayon embroidery thread and Tear-Easy stabilizer

Cutting

Square the wool and fleece and cut each into a 45" x 60" rectangle.

From the silk fabric, cut enough 3"-wide bias strips to make 220", piecing as needed. Match the design as you piece to avoid obvious seaming.

Embroidery & Felting

1 Chalk-mark the sheep placement lines along one short end of the wool, center them horizontally and position the center points 6" from the cut edge.

2 Hoop the stabilizer and fabric for the large sheep, matching the center points to the hoop markings. Stitch the outline of the sheep and remove the hoop from the machine. Do not unhoop the work. Felt roving within the outline using a single hand needle, then return the work to the machine and complete the embroidery for the head, feet and swirls. Depending on the colors used, you may want to use a topper under the face and feet area to prevent show-through of the roving. Unhoop the design and tear away the stabilizer.

Machine embroidered swirls add fun to this cute little lamb.

3 For the medium-size sheep, reduce the design size by 20% using embroidery software or on-screen editing. Hoop the stabilizer and fabric as noted above. Embroider the design, unhoop and remove the stabilizer, then felt coils of yarn within the outlined shape, following the patterning in the stitched coils. For more information on coiling, see page 37.

4 For the small sheep, reduce the design size again by 20% using embroidery software or on-screen editing. Hoop the stabilizer and fabric as noted above; embroider the design, unhoop and remove the stabilizer. Fill in the outline with felted loops using a single hand needle. For more information on making loops, see page 40.

Coiled yarns add texture.

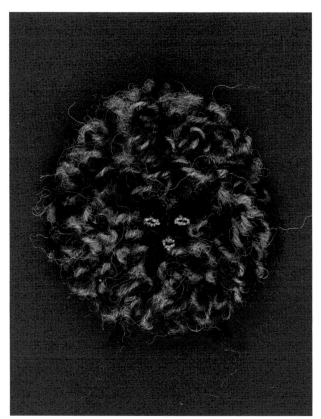

Looped yarns add dimension.

Stitch it Up

If you don't have an embroidery machine, don't despair—just use the lamb pattern on page 100 and hand or free-motion embroider the outline, face, feet and swirls for the three motifs.

If you want a different look for one of the lambs, consider felting narrow fabric strips for design fill area. For more information on this technique, see Felting Fabric on page 41.

Finishing

1 Lay the embroidered wool throw wrong side up on a flat surface and spray with temporary adhesive. Cover with the fleece right side up. Smooth the fleece into place, matching the cut edges. Baste the cut edges together ¼" from the edge.

2 If the binding fabric isn't a firm weave, fuse light-weight iron-on interfacing to the strip underside for stability.

3 Fold and press the bias binding in half, matching the cut edges.

4 Matching the cut edges, pin the bias to the throw edges right side. Stitch in place using a ¼" seam and mitering the corners as you stitch around the edges. Turn the bias to the wrong side and hand stitch in place, securing the corners as needed to maintain the miter.

Pins 'n' Needles

X

*Felt several of these quick-to-sew pincushions for all your friends.
They're a great way to try felting different types and styles of yarn
and they're sure-sellers at holiday bazaars.*

Finished size: 4½" square

MATERIALS

Two 5½" squares heavy wool

Variegated bouclé yarn

Sewing thread

Chalk marker

Polyester fiberfill*

Wave-blade scissors or rotary cutter, wave blade and mat

Felting needle, multi-needle tool or felting machine

Foam or brush base (for hand felting)

*Used in this project: Fairfield Processing, Poly-fil fiberfill

Felting

1 Chalk-mark a 4" square ¾" in from all sides of one square.

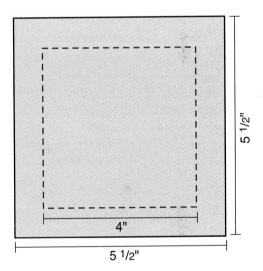

Center a design area on one wool square.

2 Randomly place the yarn within the marked square and felt in place. Tuck the yarn ends under portions of other yarns (or feather the ends, if you prefer).

3 Turn the wool over and felt from the underside to secure the yarns.

Construction

1 Place the squares wrong sides together and pin just outside the yarn-filled area.

2 Stitch on the marked lines, leaving a space open for stuffing.

3 Lightly stuff the pincushion with fiberfill and pin the opening closed.

4 Complete the stitching across the opening.

5 Use the decorative edge cutter or scissors and trim both layers of wool ¼" outside the square stitching. Gently flatten the stuffing for easier trimming.

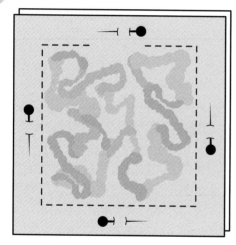

Pin outside the design area.

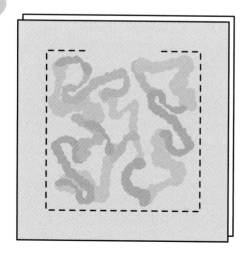

Leave open for stuffing.

Sew Many Options

- Embellish the square with a felted shape, such as the heart shown below.

- Fill the pincushion with emery to keep pins and needles sharp.

- Pack the pincushion with sand and use the square as a pattern weight.

- Stuff the square with potpourri and use as a sachet or drawer scenter.

- Use decorative stitching around the felted square.

- Trim the outer edges straight and embellish with blanket stitching.

- Make the square (or any shape) much larger and create a pillow.

Designer Terry Weiss felted this colorful heart, perfect for a pincushion center.

Button, Button

Covered buttons make wonderful accents for garments, home décor projects or craft items. They're a great way to try out novelty felting techniques on a small scale, and you can play with yarns to your heart's delight. Large button forms make great jewelry pendants.

Finished size: varies, up to 2½" diameter

MATERIALS

Cover-your-own button forms

Scraps of feltable fabrics

Assorted rovings and yarns

Felting needle, multi-needle felting tool or felting machine

Foam/brush base (for hand felting)

Chalk marker

Fusible interfacing or lining fabric (optional)

Button Forms

Cover-your-own button forms come in many sizes up to 2½" diameter. The larger ones can be used for making ornaments, craft projects and jewelry, rather than being used as operable buttons.

Some forms are metal, others are plastic, so check the notions counter to see what size and type you prefer.

Each button form consists of two pieces, a back and a front. The front has teeth around the underside to grip the felted fabric as it's stretched over it, and the back plate snaps in place to cover the raw edges. The wire shank is removable in case you want a flat back, instead of a sew-on back, for ornaments or some home décor uses.

Cover-your-own buttons come with a template of the exact fabric size needed for the assembly process. Carefully trim it from the packaging and use it as a guide for the felting process.

Felting

If you're making several buttons from the same fabric, chalk-mark the shapes onto a larger piece of fabric, leaving space between for cutting. For single buttons, cut a square of fabric about 2" larger all around than the button form pattern.

Decide on a preferred felting motif/method. Felt the area within the drawn lines of the template size, making sure to felt enough so fibers do not separate.

Felting options include twisted yarns, creating plaids with yarn strands, coiling, gauzed fibers, etc. Almost all the techniques outlined in the book will work when done on a small scale to fit covered buttons.

Finishing

1 Trim the felted fabric on the drawn template line. On fabrics that are sheer or loosely woven, back the felted fabric with a coordinating lining or fusible interfacing to prevent metallic button forms from showing through.

2 Center the button form cover on the felted fabric and, working from opposite sides, hook the taut fabric onto the underside teeth. Work around the button hooking all the fabric to the teeth. A pencil eraser can be used to make this process easier.

3 When the fabric is smoothly covering the upper button and all the teeth are holding the fabric on the underside, snap on the button backing. For thick fabrics, use a thread spool or small rubber mallet to push firmly enough to snap the backing in place.

4 Use the felted button as you would any other custom button—as a garment closure, in the center of a pillow, as an ornament, a jewelry pendant, etc.

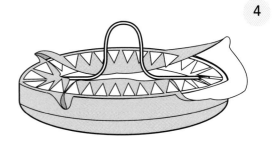

4

Stretch the fabric onto the button-back teeth.

● ● ● No-sew project!

Round About

To make the necklace shown, use a 2½" button form and coil slubby yarn within the template area of the covering fabric. Remove the wire shank before covering the button to create a flat back.

Cover the button, then sew a bead and jump ring at the top so that the pendant slides onto a neck hoop. Cover the back with felt to avoid metal against the skin, if sensitivity is an issue.

Make a whole wardrobe of pendants—the same neck hoop can be used with several different felted buttons. Just slide one off and add another.

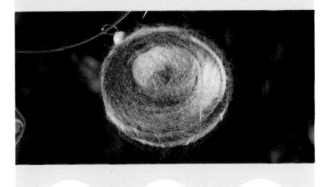

It's Ornamental

*This decorative grouping is perfect for any holiday tree
and gives you the chance to try out several different materials
and needle felting techniques.*

Finished size: 4" x 4½" tall

MATERIALS

Scraps of red and white wool coating or felt

White worsted yarn*

White and red roving

Gold yarn

Iron-on metallic star*

Stuffed heart button, 1"

Polyester fiberfill*

½ yd. red and white polka dot ribbon, ½" wide

Rubber holiday tree stamp*

Green textile paint*

Hot-fix applicator tool*

Chalk marker

Felting needle, multi-needle tool or felting machine

Foam/brush base (for hand felting)

Small foam paint brush (optional)

Tapestry needle

*Used in these projects: Caron Yarn, Wintuck, White; Fairfield Processing, Poly-fil fiberfill; Plaid Enterprises, All Night Media rubber stamp, Swash Tree 609H; Jacquard Products, Lumiere Paint #572 Pearlescent Emerald; Kandi Corp., 5mm gold star iron-on and Kandi Kane Tool

Cutting

Cut shapes from fabric at least 1" larger all around than the pattern shapes shown on page 110.

Felting

1 Chalk-mark the ornament shapes on their respective fabrics. For the star, needle felt three strands of white yarn ¼" inside the drawn line on the red fabric. For the heart, draw a line ¾" inside the inner heart edge and needle felt white roving outside the line, forming a border.

2 On the white triangle, use green paint and stamp the tree image. If there are unpainted spots due to the fuzzy fabric surface, touch up with the small foam brush; allow to dry. Using a single hand felting needle, attach the metallic braid for the garlands and felt tiny balls of red roving to create ornaments. Following the manufacturer's instructions, adhere the iron-on star at the tree top.

Finishing

1 Cut out the ornament sections on the pattern lines. Layer the inner shapes over the outer shapes and tuck in a 5" length of folded ribbon at the upper edge. For the featured heart, the underside of the felting is used as the right side. On the star and the tree, stitch just inside the inner ornament edge, catching the ribbon as you sew.

2 For the heart, use a strand of worsted yarn and blanket stitch the perimeter of the inner heart to the outer heart, leaving a small opening for stuffing (do not cut the yarn). Stuff lightly with fiberfill and continue stitching the remainder of the inner heart edge, catching the ribbon in the stitching.

3 Sew the small heart button at the center of the heart ornament.

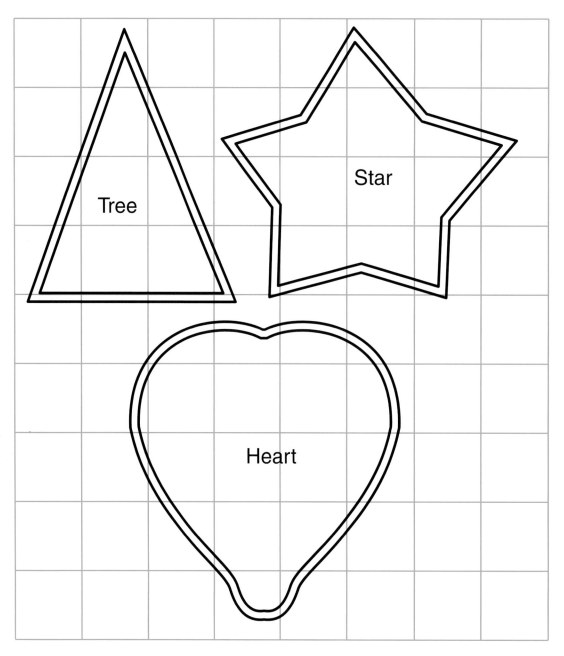

1 Square = 1 inch

On the Rocks

On the Rocks

*Keep your bubbly cool with this festive chiller cover. Ours is for Christmas,
but you could make them for any time of the year as they're removable.
Dimensional felted holly leaves and berries add interest to the flat-felted greenery.*

Finished size: cover fits a 5" diameter, 8½" tall cooler; adjust as needed

MATERIALS

7" x 18" piece of cranberry wool

Scraps of hunter green wool

Cranberry and two shades of green roving

Hunter green tapestry yarn

1⅛ yd. green gimp braid, ½" wide

6" hook-and-loop tape

Water-soluble stabilizer*

Fabric glue

Air-disappearing marker

Felting needle, multi-needle tool or felting machine

Note: Parts of this project require hand felting

Foam/brush base

Wave or pinking scissors, or rotary cutter with wave blade and mat

*Used in this project: Sulky of America, Fabri-Solvy stabilizer; Beacon Adhesives, Fabri-Tac Glue

Preparation

Using the leaf pattern on page 114, draw two leaves onto the water-soluble stabilizer. Draw a three-leaf patterning onto the center of the wool strip at 12-, 4- and 7-o'clock positions, leaving 1" open at the center.

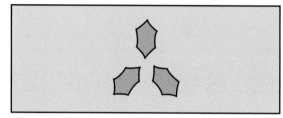

Draw the leaf positioning on the cover front.

Felting

1 For the dimensional leaves, outline the leaf drawing with roving using a single felting needle. Felt on both sides to secure the fibers. Go back and fill in the center of the leaves with lighter green roving, again felting on both sides to secure.

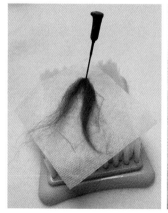
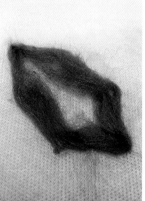

2 Fill in the veining detail with darker green yarn and go around the leaf again with a dark green yarn outline.

3 Partially dissolve the stabilizer from the leaves, leaving some in to help add body for shaping. Allow the leaves to dry.

4 Felt the three leaves on the cover following the same sequence as outlined above.

5 To make the berries, measure out three equal lengths of yarn to ensure that the berries are approximately the same diameter. Roll up the ends of yarns, untwisting as needed to loosen the fibers, and begin the needle felting process. Continue wrapping and felting the yarn length until the berries are a size you like. If you need more yarn, cut three more lengths the same size and continue felting.

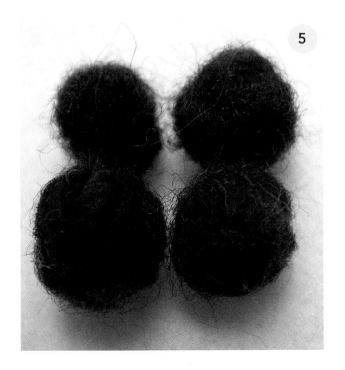

Tip

We like to make extra berries
and then pick the best shaped ones
for the project.

Finishing

1 Sew the hook-and-loop fastener tape to the short edges of the wool, forming a lapped closure to snugly hold the cover in place. Trim the overlapping fabric edge with the decorative cutting blade.

2 Glue the gimp braid to the upper and lower edges of the cover, turning under the ends to finish.

3 Lightly felt the dimensional leaves in position on the cover front, leaving some of the edges free.

4 Felt or sew the holly berries to the center leaf opening.

5 Wrap and chill, and enjoy the holidays!

Actual size

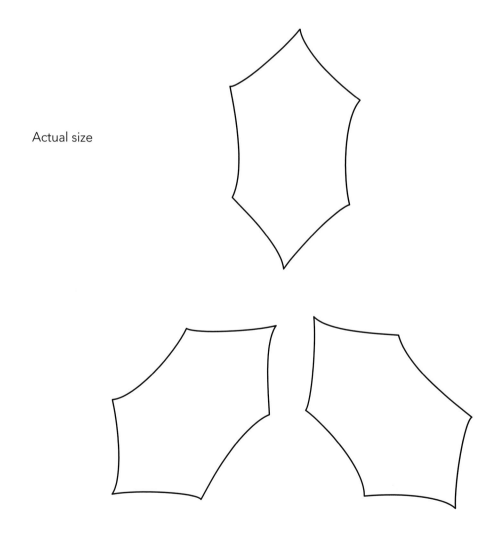

Round & Round

Round & Round

Beads are simple to make. Use a wet-felting technique along with needle felting to create a firm, round shape. Pick some wonderful glass beads as spacers and coordinate the felted beads with the shiny highlights.

Finished size: 15" long

MATERIALS

Note: Materials and beads may vary depending on the desired finished look.

5 dichroic glass beads, ¾" long

18 metallic spacer beads, ³⁄₁₆" diameter

Assorted colors of wool roving

1 yd. thin silk cord

Tapestry needle

Sewing/beading thread

Single felting needle

Foam/brush base

Liquid soap (not detergent)

Note: Beads need to be hand-felted.

Felting

1 Begin the beadmaking process with approximately the same amount of roving for each bead needed if you want them to be similar sizes. For variation, make the beads different sizes.

2 Roll the roving into a ball and needle felt to hold it together. Using a small drop of soap in warm water, wet the felted roving. Roll the balls several times, felting as you work until they are the approximate size you want. Rinse and allow to dry thoroughly.

3 Add more roving or yarns to the beads to create the patterning you want (stripes, dots, color blendings, etc.) and needle felt in place.

Finishing

1 Thread the beads onto the silk cord in the desired sequence using the spacers between the glass beads and felted beads.

2 Try on the necklace and determine the preferred finished length. Cut and tie the cord in a double knot.

3 To make the center front multi-bead hanging, use sewing or beading thread to sew an additional bead to the center bead, followed by another glass bead and two spacers. Come back up through all the beads with the thread to anchor them in place.

Shepherdess and fiber artist Jan McMahon combined wet felting and needle felting to create these beautiful necklaces. Swarovski crystal beads highlight the matte texture of the felted surfaces.

Designer Sandra Ahlgren Sapienza combined novelty yarns with roving and beads to fashion this multi-media art work entitled "The Wise Woman's Eye." From the collection of Arlinka Blair.

Gallery

Sometimes being inspired is all it takes to kick-start your creative juices.
We've asked some talented needle felters to share their work with you,
and we hope you use it for inspiration in your own original works.
Look for other artists' creations throughout the text.

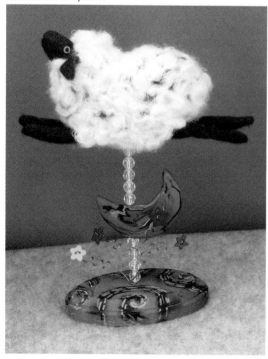

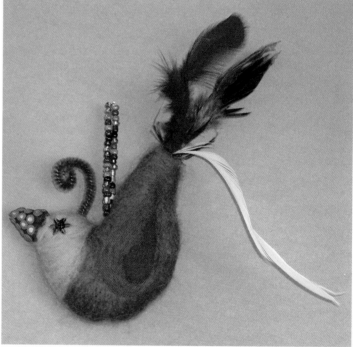

"Leaping Sheepy"

A stuffed muslin base is the beginning of
this cute soft sculpture kit designed by Anne
Boyer for Fanatica Fibers.

"Fall Bird Ornament"

Designer Ann Boyer shows off whimsical needle felting with
her Fanatica Fibers fall bird kit.

Pat Spark photos

"Budapest Rhodie"

Fiber artist Pat Spark needle felted this beautiful rhododendron using merino wool on a merino wool base.

Clotilde's Sewing Savvy photo

Baby Lock photo

Pat Spark photo

Designer Chris Tryon used a felting machine to pierce the silk pillow center along drawn gridlines to texturize it, then felted yarns to highlight the border.

"Brooklyn: Disparate Parrot"

A single-layer vest showcases a single needle felted flower and wispy leaves created with rovings. Designed by Pauline Richards.

Fiber artist Pat Spark used a wet felted wool base to needle felt the colorful parrot.

Designer Kathryn Brenne used colorful hand-dyed wool rovings to embellish this fall coat. In addition, she machine washed and dried the wool crepe base to shrink it before felting.

Doug Brenne photos

Pat Spark photos

"Oriental Poppies"

Fiber artist Pat Spark created these bright flowering poppies with merino wool on a merino wool base.

*House of White Birches,
"Easy Embellishments" photo*

Designer Pauline Richards used color blocking highlights on this beautiful felted bag. For more information on this technique, see On the Flip Side on page 73.

"Amazon Froggie"

Needle felting and appliqué techniques combine to create this fun quilt knitted by My Favorite Thimble designer Chris Hanner.

Designer Melissa Brown's simple clutch is highlighted with funky multi-color yarn machine felted to the flap for instant pizzazz!

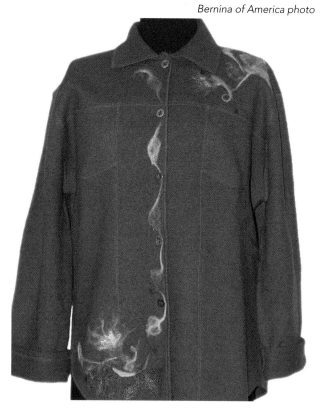

"Conga Line"

Chris Hanner, owner of My Favorite Thimble, designed this bright 24" x 36" needle felted quilt kit.

Feathery roving and yarn flowers highlight Nancy Bednar's wool jacket. Notice the eye is lead to the face by the shoulder motifs.

Bernina of America photos

Designer Kerry Finn's jackets use slubby yarns and more twisted yarns to create visual texture and embellishment on solid-color wool bases.

Baby Lock photo

Brother International photo

Dancing Needleworks photo

"Julia's Garden"

Designer Tricia Anderson machine felted hand-dyed wools in place, then accented the finished piece with free-motion stitchery using 12-weight thread.

Fleece is always a popular option and Baby Lock designer Kelly Laws used both felt shapes and yarns to machine felt this sporty jacket and scarf.

Meandering multi-color yarns accent Kathy McMannis' cozy berber jacket.

"Red Posy"

Designer Margo Duke machine felted unusual materials combined with wool roving for her vest and purse combo.

"Little Ron"

Artist Mary Burt sculpted Ron using a combination of wet felting and dimensional needle felting techniques over a wire armature, so he's totally posable. Note the fine facial details done with single-needle felting—this expert work is something to aspire to! Design by Deborah Pope.

"Grand Canyon"

Designer Shirley Biehl crafted this landscape of the Grand Canyon on faux suede using rovings and novelty yarns, then stretched it on a frame for hanging.

Designers

Many thanks to the following designers who shared their work with us throughout this book:

Dorothy Akiyama, Tricia Anderson, Nancy Bednar, Marlis Bennett, Shirley Biehl, Anne Boyer, Kathyrn Brenne, Melissa Brown, Mary Burt, Margo Duke, Kerry Finn, Chris Hanner, Kelly Laws, Jo Leichte, Kathy McMannis, Jan McMahon, Nina McVeigh, Faith Reynolds, Laura Rintala, Sandra Ahlgren Sapienza, Pat Spark, Alyce Thomson, Chris Tryon, Terry Weiss.

Resources

Many, many companies sell needle felting fibers and supplies.
Those marked with an asterisk below contributed product or samples to this book – thank you!

Fibers/Yarns

Coats & Clark*
800-648-1479
www.coatsandclark.com
Yarns and novelty threads

Conjoined Creations*
480-488-0324
www.ConjoinedCreations.com
Soy Silk

DMC*
973-589-0606
www.dmc-usa.com
Tapestry wool, assorted yarns and
floss

Lion Brand Yarns*
800-258-YARN (9276)
www.lionbrand.com
Assorted yarns

The Spinning Ewe Farm*
503-632-3354
www.spinningewe.com
Hand-dyed yarns and roving

Westminster Fibers
800-445-9276
www.westminsterfibers.com
Nashua yarns

Needle Felting Supplies

Clover Needlecraft*
562-282-0200
www.clover-usa.com
Tools and brush mats

Colonial Needle*
800-963-3353/914-946-7474
www.colonialneedle.com
Tools, fibers

Dancing Needleworks*
www.dancingneedleworks.com
Patterns, tools, fibers

Fanatica Fibers*
www.fanaticafibers.com
Soft sculpture and ornament kits

Feltcrafts*
800-450-2723/607-423-4023
www.feltcrafts.com
Tools, fibers, books, kits

Indygo Junction/The Vintage
Workshop*
877-546-3946/913-341-5559
www.indygojunction.com
www.thevintageworkshop.com
Patterns, tools, fibers,
inkjet printable fabrics

Lacis
510-843-7178
www.lacis.com
Tools, fibers, books, kits

My Favorite Thimble*
770-978-5671
www.myfavoritethimble.com
Colonial Needle tools, fibers, kits

National Nonwovens*
800-333-3469/413-527-3445
www.nationalnonwovens.com
ShadedWisps, WoolWisps

Nancy's Notions*
800-833-0690
www.nancysnotions.com
Tools, fibers

Shirley's Sewing Stuff*
800-375-2785/812-683-3377
www.shirleyssewingstuff.com
Tools

The Sewing Connection
800-237-4475
www.sewingconnection.com
Patterns, fibers, needles

WizPick*
www.wizpick.com
Felting needles

Woolcombs.com*
604-463-4744
www.woolcombs.com
Handmade hardwood felting
tools

Needle Felting
Machines/Attachments

Baby Lock (Embellisher)*
800-422-2952
www.babylock.com

Bernina*
800-669-1647
www.berninausa.com

Brother*
800-422-7684
www.brothersews.com

Feltcrafts*
800-450-2723/607-423-4023
www.feltcrafts.com

Husqvarna Viking*
(Husky-Star ER10)
800-358-0001
www.husqvarnaviking.com

Janome (Xpression)*
800-631-0183/201-825-3300
www.janome.com

Nancy's Notions (Sewing with Nancy Fab Felter)*
800-833-0690
www.nancysnotions.com

Pfaff (Smart 350P)
800-997-3233
www.pfaff.com

Project Supplies

Beacon Adhesives*
914-699-3405
www.beaconadhesives.com
Fabri-Tac Glue

Cactus Punch*
800-933-8081
www.cactuspunch.com
Machine embroidery designs

Colonial Patterns
816-471-3313
www.colonialpatterns.com
Aunt Martha's Iron-on Transfers

Crafter's Pick*
510-526-7616
www.crafterspick.com
Crafter's Pick The Ultimate! Glue

Floriani*
877-331-0034
www.RNKdistributing.com
Stitch N Shape craft interfacing

Jacquard Products*
800-442-0455/707-433-9577
www.jacquardproducts.com
Fabric paints

June Tailor*
800-844-5400/262-644-5288
www.junetailor.com
Mix 'n Match templates for Quilters

Kandi Corp.*
800-895-2634/727-441-4100
www.kandicorp.com
Kandi Kane hot-fix applicator,
iron-ons

Klaer International*
203-322-5123
needlethreaders@aol.com,
Needle threaders

MacPhee Workshop*
888-622-7433
www.machpheeworkshop.com
Wool melton and coating duffle
fabrics

Olfa*
800-962-6532
www.olfa.com
Rotary cutters and decorative
blades

Plaid Enterprises
800-842-4197
www.plaidonline.com
Simply Stencils, All Night Media
rubber stamps

ScrapSmart*
800-424-1011/585-424-5300
www.scrapsmart.com
Inkjet printable imagery

Stitchery Safe*
801-521-7566
www.tennews.homestead.com
My Favorite Vest pattern

Sulky of America*
800-874-4115
www.sulky.com
Embroidery threads, KK2000
Temporary Spray Adhesive, Tear-
Easy and Fabri-Solvy Stabilizers

Textura Trading Company
877-839-8872
www.texturatrading.com
Angelina fibers

The Warm Company*
800-234-9276
www.warmcompany.com
Warm & Natural Batting, Steam-
A-Seam2 Paper-back Fusible
Web

YLI Corp.
803-985-3100
www.ylicorp.com
Glow-in-the-dark threads

Publications

Clotilde's Sewing Savvy*
800-449-0440
www.clotildessewingsavvy.com

House of White Birches*
800-829-5865
"Easy Embellishments for Creative Sewing"
www.drgbooks.com

Krause Publications
800-829-0929
www.krausebooks.com

Other Web Sites of Interest to Needle Felters

www.blacksheepdesigns.com
www.chocolatesheepgallery.com
www.colonialcrafts.com/
needlefelting
www.earthsongfibers.com
www.feltdesigns.com
www.fiberella.com
www.hookedonfelt.com
www.joggles.com
www.livingfelt.com
www.mielkesfarm.com
www.moondancecolor.com
www.sparkfiberarts.com
www.woolery.com
www.wysteria.com

About the Authors

Linda Turner Griepentrog

Linda was the editor of *Sew News* magazine for 19 years, and currently owns G Wiz Creative Services (so named because no one can pronounce her last name).

Linda writes, edits, plays and sews for a number of companies in the sewing and craft industries. In addition, she leads fabric shopping tours to various destinations in the U.S. and abroad. Once a weaver (and now wishing she had time to do it), Linda loves fibers and needle felting lets her play with them in another way. Working from her basement office, Linda lives outside Portland, Oregon, with her husband, Keith, and two dogs, Riley and Buckley. Contact Linda at gwizdesigns@aol.com.

Pauline Wilde Richards

Pauline has been sewing since she was a child. She has taught clothing construction at the high school and college levels and is the publisher of *Total Embellishment Newsletter*, a quarterly newsletter for creative sewing and embellishment enthusiasts. For the past 13 years she has worked as a freelance writer and teacher. Her work has been featured in *Sew News*, *Creative Machine Embroidery* and *Better Homes and Gardens Creative Home*. She is known for her innovative techniques, practical advice and ability to convert leftover fabrics and trims into spectacular, one-of-a-kind wearables. Pauline is a proud grandmother who lives in Salt Lake City, Utah, with her husband, John, children and Powder, the family dog. Contact Pauline at sewnocooking@aol.com.

Look for other Krause Publications titles by Linda —

Embroidery Machine Essentials: Quilting Techniques

Machine Embroidery Wild & Wacky
(co-authored with Rebecca Kemp Brent)

Print Your Own Fabric
(co-authored with Missy Shepler)

More Ways to Make the Most of Your Sewing Skills

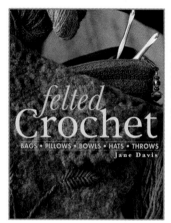

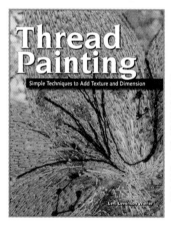
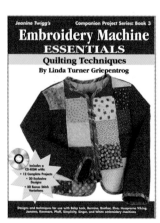